The
hands and feet of Jesus

Text copyright © Clive Price 2007, except Questions for discussion and reflection
© Jonathan Francis 2007
The author asserts the moral right
to be identified as the author of this work

Published by
The Bible Reading Fellowship
First Floor, Elsfield Hall
15–17 Elsfield Way, Oxford OX2 8FG
Website: www.brf.org.uk

ISBN 978 1 84101 508 8
First published 2007
10 9 8 7 6 5 4 3 2 1 0
All rights reserved

Acknowledgments
Scripture quotations taken from the Holy Bible, New International Version, copyright
© 1973, 1978, 1984 by International Bible Society, are used by permission of
Hodder & Stoughton Publishers, a division of Hodder Headline Ltd. All rights
reserved. 'NIV' is a registered trademark of International Bible Society. UK trademark
number 1448790.

Scripture quotations marked (NLT) are taken from the Holy Bible, New Living
Translation, copyright © 1996. Used by permission of Tyndale House Publishers,
Inc., Wheaton, Illinois 60189. All rights reserved.

Scripture quotations from THE MESSAGE. Copyright © by Eugene H. Peterson 1993,
1994, 1995. Used by permission of NavPress Publishing Group.

A catalogue record for this book is available from the British Library

Printed in Singapore by Craft Print International Ltd

The
hands and feet of Jesus

Stories of ordinary people doing extraordinary things

Clive Price

Acknowledgments

It was an ambitious idea, and without the help of countless people across the globe, it would have never happened.

First of all, Peter Scott called and said, 'We want to gather stories from World Vision teams in different nations and put them into one book—will you write it?' I said, 'Yes.' I thought it would slip into a comfortable slot in my work schedule. Then it took over the schedule.

But there wasn't a dull moment. Every story had power and impact. Each account took me to a different place in my imagination—from arid wastelands to enchanted lakes, from battlefields to pleasant meadows. Amy Polson kept tabs on the material and continued to feed the stories through for me to write.

There were others behind the scenes, such as communications officers and staff writers—some who supplied raw material and others who checked the facts and read through the text. Jonathan Francis offered input from his own publishing background. The wonderful Naomi Starkey was the anchorperson at BRF.

Thanks go to them all for their loyal support, but most important of all, thanks to the people whose stories made it into the finished product. They are on the frontline while we are in the queue at the supermarket. They are in barren places while we relax in the local park. They face conflict while we enjoy peace.

Their stories challenge us all to have a vision for our world.

Contents

Foreword 6

Introduction: Visionaries for the world 11

1   The Celtic tiger 16

2   History maker 23

3   New morning 30

4   One peace at a time 37

5   Place of miracles 44

6   Out of the 'sacred house' 50

7   Shaking the holy ground 57

8   Knocked off my feet 63

9   Their eyes speak more than any words 71

10 The people who touch the sky 78

11 Fighting the new apartheid 84

12 Priest of the muddy paths 90

13 Child of the killing fields 96

14 Make my life count 103

15 A table in the wilderness 110

16 Hope in the highlands 117

17 The chocolate man 124

Questions for discussion and reflection 131

✧

Foreword

In January 2000 my wife Bridget and I travelled to Bangladesh to look at the work that World Vision is doing in that country and to meet Shahnaj, our sponsored child. One specific aim of that trip was to discover for ourselves if child sponsorship actually works. On our return we produced a book entitled *Colours of Survival* (Marshall Pickering). In 2004 we made a second trip, this time to the African nation of Zambia, and in particular to the poverty-stricken community of Zamtan. Our brief on this occasion was to look at projects connected with HIV and AIDS and to meet some of those who have been affected directly or indirectly by this terrible modern plague. A second book, *The Son of God is Dancing* (Authentic, 2005), resulted from this journey.

These two volumes of ours may be slight, but they are filled with passion, people and examples of practical love. I find it interesting that when Bridget and I are asked to sum up or crystallize our experiences in these two different countries, we invariably find ourselves referring to a conclusion that is expressed in the closing chapters of both books. *The Son of God is Dancing* puts it like this:

In Zamtan there were no Exodus-type miracles going on. No flocks of quail dropping from the sky, or manna raining down from heaven. Most people were hungry for much of the time. As far as we could see there were no dramatic healings happening in this community either. The people who suffered from AIDS, for instance, continued to suffer from that dread disease. They will suffer even more, and die sooner, without the provision of expensive, complex drugs. It was the same when we visited the slums of Dhaka in Bangladesh. The love of God was only being expressed in those endless acres of desolation to the extent that people were willing to practically serve those who were in need. Do not misunderstand me. I believe in miracles. I really do. And I know that they can happen anywhere and at any time. But when you are standing in these places, when you walk up and down the dusty trails of poverty-stricken, disease-ridden communities, you know—you just know—that the first call of God on those who claim to care is the same call that was received by Mother Teresa. It is the call to be his hands and feet. God with skin on, as someone once put it. Whether it is by going or by giving or by getting practically involved in some other way, we can be part of the sacrificial, generous love of the risen Jesus reaching out to a fallen, hurting world through his body on earth. Perhaps that will turn out to be the greatest miracle of all.

We shall never forget the many people we met who were responding to that call by taking the love of God to those who needed it most.

We remember two women in the slums of Dhaka, one Christian and one Muslim, who were running a World Vision project designed to help young girls living in the slums. Most of these children are without parents, without love and without any means of feeding or supporting themselves. Some are forced into prostitution at a very young age. We heard of one little scrap who began to sell her body at the age of six, and was worn out and dead soon after reaching her eighth birthday.

The project run by these two women takes girls off the street and enables them to have a shower and put on a beautiful clean blue dress. As a group they eat together, enjoy games, play musical instruments and take part in little dramas that are designed to bring a new understanding into their lives. The most important thing they need to comprehend, we were told, is what it means to be 'normal'. For those who have been used and abused and half starved for the whole of their short lives, this is not an easy lesson to learn. Imagine how the sorrowing heart of God must be warmed by the gradual appearance of a new light in the eyes of these precious little ones as they grasp the astonishing fact that there may be something in them that is worth loving.

We remember Father Parimal Rozario, a Roman Catholic priest who was our host and guide in the rural district of Tuital. Father Parimal was a quietly confident, even-featured man who had his own very particular approach to solving the problems involved in ministering the Christian faith in a Muslim community. The previous priest had been threatened and severely intimidated by militant, violently anti-Christian Muslims and forced to live in a state of virtual siege.

'When I came here,' said our host, as we ate dinner together on the second day of our stay, 'I made a point of walking straight into the home of the leading Muslim troublemaker, and I said to him, "What is all this I hear about attacking Christians? Show me around, and then make me a cup of tea and tell me about it." So he showed me everything and we drank tea and became friends. He was no more trouble after that.'

He went on to tell us of the secret desire of many Muslims to become Christians, and their fear that if they did so they would have to leave home for good, for fear of being killed.

'The work and generosity of World Vision,' continued the priest, 'provides a bridge to the Muslim community which makes it much easier for me to cross over. The people have received and are grateful. I am able to tell them who they should be grateful to.'

There were theological differences between Father Parimal and ourselves, and we find the Roman Catholic teaching on birth control difficult to accept in the context of countries such as Bangladesh, but in one sense none of that matters. When I asked this man how he felt about Jesus, his face became illuminated by the kind of smile that is born out of contact with God. As we discovered during our stay, he was patently loved and respected by adults and children alike, and he was simply there, in this dangerous and challenging situation, doing the job that God had given him to do. He deserves our love and respect, and we shall leave God to sort out the theology.

As we look back to our African trip, we remember Phyllis Chintu, a trained nurse who heads up the Zamtan Home Care team, a group of women who, as local volunteers, visit and physically care for those who suffer from AIDS. This devoted group of women spend their time engaged in such activities as cleaning wounds and mopping up vomit. Although generously supported by World Vision and other agencies, their supply of medicine and drugs is sadly limited.

Because of the expense and complexity involved in administering the anti-retroviral drugs that can combat the effects of AIDS, there is none available for use in Zamtan. The Home Care team simply do what they can, bringing strong antibiotics to their clients and working hard to ensure that patients actually take their medicine. Phyllis explained: 'We take salt and mix it with water to bathe wounds. We give medicine to soothe coughs. We sweep the floor and bathe the children. We do whatever is necessary and possible, but we wish we could do more.'

Phyllis introduced us to Mankina, who had been part of the team from the very beginning. Now in her 70s, this woman, tiny in stature and wrinkled with age, is tireless. She gets up at 5.30 every morning so that she can visit the houses of sufferers and report to the team on who is most urgently in need of a visit.

'Also,' Phyllis said, 'she tells us who has passed away in the night. That is very depressing, you know. Every day there is some heartbreak in Zamtan.'

God bless Phyllis and Mankina and all the other women in this team for their dedication, their hard work and their commitment to suffering people who come last in the eyes of the world and are therefore first in the merciful heart of God.

So many other remarkable characters spring to mind.

Emmanuel was a gently spoken Zambian man, tall, emaciated and large-eyed, who had adopted nine children orphaned as a result of AIDS. He worked quietly and continually for the good of his community, accepting in return a single bag of maize each month to assist in the making of *nshima*, the flavourless porridge that constitutes the staple diet of many Zambians. Emmanuel will never write a testimony paperback or become a speaker at Christian conferences, but he is honoured by God for his unselfishness and service to others.

Particularly memorable for us was a woman who goes regularly on behalf of World Vision to talk to lorry drivers stranded by red tape in the no-man's-land that is the Kasumbalesa border crossing between Zambia and the Congo. Known to sex workers and lorry drivers alike as Auntie Doris, this five-foot colossus good-humouredly challenges men who appear to be twice her size about the dangers of their lifestyle, the need to use condoms, and the lethal consequences of passing on the HIV virus through unprotected sex. It has to be seen to be believed. God sees it and loves her for what she does. We are quite sure that Auntie Doris is one of the 'big names' in heaven. Thank God that there are people who are willing, courageous and obedient enough to follow Jesus into such a place and to undertake such a task.

What is the point of it all?

Perhaps that question is best answered with one more recollection. In the course of our Bangladesh trip we were introduced to a group of very enthusiastic and appreciative women who had been helped by World Vision workers to form a village savings group. 'Tell me,' I asked, 'why do you think these workers come and help you to set up schemes like this? Why would they do that?'

There was a pause, and then one of the women said something in her language that triggered loud agreement from the others. When the translation came, it was only four words, but they were four golden words. 'World Vision loves us.'

This love, expressed through World Vision as well as through many other Christian agencies, is the passion and compassion of Jesus, reaching out through the hands of his obedient servants. That is what this book is about.

Adrian Plass

✝

Visionaries for the world

As the world's spotlight turned on him, Irish rock star Bono turned his spotlight on the world. U2, the young band that he fronted, was climbing and about to enter the stratosphere. But this experience was very down to earth.

He received a phone call from Steve Reynolds of World Vision, inviting him to Ethiopia. The Dublin rocker responded. He and his wife Ali went to work as volunteers in a World Vision nutrition centre. Steve remembers it vividly:

Far different from the many celebrities and 'notables' who passed through the World Vision office at that time—mainly only to 'see and be seen' as taking an interest—Bono and Ali came to stay, to work and to pour themselves out for people who were starving to death before our eyes.

They stayed in extremely basic conditions in tents and makeshift shelters made of wood and tin, eating the local food, and building the trust of the Ethiopian staff and clients.

The couple lived and worked in Ajibar, on a barren, windswept plateau in the central highlands. Bono and Ali wrote songs and dramas for the children and adults staying in the centre, where several thousand were receiving medical care, intensive feeding for malnourished youngsters and food rations for families.

Bono was asked many years later, on the Oprah Winfrey Show, why he took the time and effort to go to Ethiopia: 'I just did what anybody else would do who had the time and the money to go.' But it set him on a pilgrimage that has taken him from a mud hut to a White House in search of help for Africa's people.

Since then, Bono has campaigned for a heartfelt, practical response to the continent's needs. In 2002 his quest took him on the *Heart Of America* tour, when he called the church in the USA to respond compassionately to Africa's AIDS crisis. Steve Reynolds met up with him again at one of the dates.

It was a treat for me to reconnect with the man I first saw standing in the lobby of the Ethiopia Hotel in 1985 during the greatest human tragedy of that time. Today we are engaged in yet another human tragedy… the tragedy of AIDS, and indeed a potentially even more difficult battle… the battle against judgment and indifference.

As we talked, I sensed the same sense of passion and commitment that drove Bono to the remotest parts of Ethiopia to help those on the brink of survival gleam in his bright sunglass-covered eyes. He has not lost an ounce of that drive or determination.

Igniting that spark is what World Vision does. Its approach to development work is to build a constituency of people, both in the developing communities and in the UK, Australia, Canada, USA and elsewhere. Then together they can make a difference.

Today World Vision works in nearly 100 countries. It means that in numerous regions across the globe, World Vision is able to support ordinary people to climb out of the pit of poverty. It does that through area development programmes (ADPs), through setting up local community-based organizations (CBOs) and through responding to natural and manmade disasters.

An ADP is a long-term, locally managed project that enables poor communities to target the root of their problems. Largely funded by World Vision's child sponsorship programme, ADPs are owned and directed by the people themselves. Globally, World Vision today supports around 1500 of these integrated and sustainable projects, which help families gain access to things like clean water, long-term food sources, health care, education and economic opportunities.

A CBO can be any local group, from a women's association to a village well committee. They ensure that local institutions are in place to carry the work forward and eventually take over from World Vision. However, efforts may initially be focused on a disaster zone highlighted in the media. World Vision is often among the first agencies on the scene, but World Vision and its associates remain long after the journalists have left for the next story. The response to the devastating tsunami that hit the coastlines of south Asia in 2004 is a case in point.

The Revd Christine Musser, featured in BBC TV's *A Seaside Parish*, went to see how communities in Thailand had been coping since the tsunami. She knows something about the damage that water can do: her parish includes the floodswept town of Boscastle in Cornwall.

We were so fortunate in Boscastle [she comments]. No lives were lost, but we felt a strong connection with the people of south-east Asia... During the trip to Thailand, I met many people whose lives had been totally turned upside down by the tsunami. But it was very encouraging to see people beginning to recover their lives and to witness first-hand the vital work that agencies like World Vision are doing.

Such programmes can result in dramatic changes to local landscapes, both physically and spiritually, as people from different backgrounds and beliefs work together to restore their communities.

Meanwhile, Evangelical Alliance general director Joel Edwards travelled to India with World Vision UK's chief executive Charles Badenoch, and found 'living hope' in the tsunami-hit villages of India. Joel recalls their visit to the stricken state of Tamil Nadu:

In the UK I find people struggling to define hope. During my trip to India, hope became palpable, became touchable. It was on people's faces, inside and outside the temporary accommodation I visited. It was inscribed in the faces of children moments after they were telling me devastating stories of the death of their parents. And it was made real through the endurance of people's aspirations for the future.

Joel and Charles made the journey to see first-hand how some of the £400 million raised by the British public was enabling communities in India to recover. Charles explains how they saw World Vision's ideal of 'connecting people' come alive:

The wave left more than 10,000 people dead and thousands more homeless. But it was soon followed by a huge wave of generosity and support from the British public, enabling agencies such as World Vision to respond within hours of the disaster. And now support is helping communities to build back better.

Nearly 3000 had been killed on the Beach Road market area of Nagapattinam. But when they talked with some of the locals, Joel and Charles did not find people crippled with anger or despair. They actually found Hindus, Muslims and Christians being supported by World Vision and being united in the common cause of restoration. 'The tsunami has become a connector between faiths,' they were told.

When the England cricket team heard about the tsunami, they wanted to donate money to support children directly affected, so they gave £20,000 to World Vision's Tsunami Response Child Protection Programme in Sri Lanka, working with communities to protect the rights of children who were affected.

World Vision can operate in a way that is sensitive to local cultures because it is not one single entity shut away in an office block away from the main action. Its structure operates as a partnership of interdependent national bases. A common mission statement and shared core values bind the partnership offices together. But this unique network co-ordinates strategic operations and represents World Vision in the international arena.

It is a team spirit, through and through, and that 'connecting' value was highlighted behind the scenes of the tsunami appeal, when countless ordinary people gave generously to help the relief effort. They included boys from Bedford Prep School, who organized a number of fund-raising activities from a cake stall to a concert and made nearly £1400. Three Counties Radio heard about it and a live link-up was set up between the school and Sri Lanka. The pupils heard from the survivors themselves.

Speaking out for the vulnerable is another facet of World Vision's work. While individual programmes can tackle the effects of poverty, World Vision believes that it is only by standing up for the marginalized that the underlying causes can be dealt with. So, by promoting justice and campaigning for the poor, it addresses the complex systematic factors that perpetuate poverty.

A visible manifestation of that could be seen during the Make Poverty History initiative in 2005. World Vision played its part in lobbying the government and mobilizing public support for events such as the G8 rally in Edinburgh. Just before the G8 Summit, it helped to sponsor a Make Poverty History conference in London. World Vision's recently appointed Campaigns Manager Ashley Riley helped to co-ordinate some of those strategic steps towards a better future for poorer communities. 'We are campaigning to change things—not simply win hearts and minds,' he said.

This collection of stories from across the global partnership is part of that process. It is both a celebration and an exhortation—to stand up and be counted. Throughout this volume, you will find accounts from various 'frontlines'. Whether they are working in disaster zones or fund-raising on the streets, we can share in the experiences of fellow workers, partners and supporters across the globe.

Back to Bono to sum it all up: 'This is our moment, this is our time, this is our chance to stand up for what is right.' Let us all reflect on the urgency and the opportunity as we read these stories —and celebrate.

Chapter 1

The Celtic tiger

Volcanoes, hurricanes and armed rebels are occupational hazards
for Sheila Donaghy. This Irish nurse and national emergencies
seem to go together.

It was like getting ready to fly into the eye of a storm. News had just
broken of the genocide that had ripped Rwanda apart, and Irish
nurse Sheila Donaghy was preparing to go there.

She had only just returned from Romania. There, she had worked
at a terminal care unit for children with HIV and AIDS, where she
had to have a supply of nails and a hammer on her desk to seal
coffins. Sheila explains:

*I felt my experiences in Romania would prove beneficial to me in Rwanda.
I'd experienced poverty, extreme suffering and loss—and I had dealt a lot
with death. So in a sense, I felt as prepared as I could be.*

*The scenes we were seeing on our TV sets were dead bodies floating in
Lake Kivu and being washed up along the shorelines—and the shocked
and vacant faces of thousands of women and children.*

The international community had ignored the horror that had deci-
mated the Central African country. Between April and July 1994,
more than 800,000 ethnic Tutsis and moderate Hutus had been
murdered. The atrocities had been revealed partly by World Vision
communications staff. They had filmed the gruesome realities first-
hand, including a church in which hundreds of men, women and
children had been brutally murdered.

Sheila moved to this wounded land in September 1994. Based at a World Vision Unaccompanied Children's Centre (UCC), she was working with children who had been separated from, or had lost, their families:

They were living 'alone' in camps or on the streets, so they came to the centres for health care/shelter/education/tracing their families—and hopefully being reunited with their loved ones.

I was there until November 1995. It was a challenge, because there was so much mistrust and fear. In the genocide, groups that had previously been living alongside each other started to kill each other... It was difficult to know who you were employing—anyone could have been a killer.

The best times were when they reunited families. Sometimes, however, they would return to a village only to find everything destroyed and the children's hopes shattered. Yet, amid the terror, Sheila saw forgiveness in action. It made her think, 'What right do I have to be angry on his or her behalf?'

On one occasion, she was interviewing people to work in a centre. Among the candidates was a local girl in her early 20s. It was clear she had some deep needs. Shaking and twitching, the young woman couldn't look anyone in the eye. Sheila takes up the story:

She said she was called Beatrice. I found out much later that she wasn't! Local authorities had given us a list of candidates to interview. She had somehow seen the list and had memorized a name from there.

I really felt that I should give her a job, so she began to work in the laundry. Within two weeks she was laughing and talkative. She had transformed so much that she ended up being a children's worker at the centre.

Sheila happened to attend a local church meeting and found the new worker there. 'Beatrice' stood up to share something. 'I thank God for the gift of life,' she said, 'and I thank World Vision for a job, as now I have life.'

Her story was intense in its drama and emotion. When militia invaded her village, Beatrice had knelt to pray. The intruders asked what she was doing. When she told them, they asked why. They said the God of the Tutsis was dead. Then they attacked her with a machete and left her for dead.

The militia were barbarians. They killed some but maimed many others. They would leave the victims bleeding and unable to walk, then threaten to return and finish them off a few days later. It was psychological torture. Sheila tells us:

Thinking she was already dead, someone threw her into a mass grave. But then some other soldiers came, saw her move and rescued her. So her thanking God for the gift of life was really something, considering what she'd been through.

I learnt never to give up on anyone, or yourself. When there's breath, there's hope and a future.

Sheila's time in Rwanda ended in November 1995. But that's not the only challenging situation she has encountered—far from it. Her CV reads like a directory of disaster regions, war zones and national emergencies. As well as Romania and Rwanda, she has worked in Honduras during the time of Hurricane Mitch; among the Roma people of Montenegro; in the aftermath of Afghanistan's Taliban regime; amid rebels and volcanoes in the Congo; in the unstable environment of Iraq and in Sudan, Uganda, Kenya and Tanzania.

In Honduras, she was even registered as a missing person. Her Irish government-backed team knew she was in town, but all she could do was wait out the arrival of the hurricane. So she spent a night in a hotel with stranded tourists, listening to the winds and rains and waiting for it all to pass over. Chaos ensued, with communication breakdown, looting and stranded survivors. As soon as the airport reopened, Sheila flew to the north coast to help out there, but she had no way of letting her colleagues know that she was all right. She recalls: 'I was six weeks on the "missing" register.

When I eventually arrived back in La Esperanza, various ladies in the bank, the post office and the market all remarked that they thought I was dead. We had a happy reunion.'

After Honduras, she worked on a World Vision health education programme with the Roma people of Montenegro who had fled from Kosovo. 'This was a challenge,' she says; 'they were very untrusting.'

The people had little education, so everything Sheila did had to be shown practically. Eventually they listened, and Sheila asked them why. 'Because you came into our houses,' they replied, 'drank tea from our cups and listened to us.' That taught her the importance of meeting with individuals where they are and starting with what they understand. 'Respect is a two-way process,' says Sheila.

The cultural challenges were even greater in Afghanistan in 2002. She was working in a nutrition programme for children under five and pregnant or breastfeeding mothers, but she found that she was a woman in a man's world.

According to Sheila, there was little health care for women under the Taliban. Male doctors were not allowed to see or touch the women, and women themselves weren't allowed to be doctors:

The pecking order was men—male children—female children—animals —women. In family cars, women sat in the boot. When I was invited to eat with families, I had to sit a certain distance away from the men. The women were preparing food in a different area and weren't allowed in the room.

If I wanted to meet them I had to go round the back, escorted by a male relative. The translator—who would always have been male—wasn't allowed with me to see the women. So I couldn't talk to them at all.

Sheila also worked on a nutrition programme in the Democratic Republic of Congo. Rebel activity made travel risky—it seemed as if there was a bandit round every corner—and Sheila was the first white person to live in her village. Suddenly, the volcano at Goma started to erupt. There was smoke everywhere, and people feared for their lives. Sheila and her team decided to join the other villagers and pack as much as they could to cross the border into Rwanda:

It turned out to be just a small eruption, so we soon returned. Some days later, on New Year's Day, we were returning from a field visit when we ran into bandits. We were held up at gunpoint. But we soon realized that the bandits were drunk—and just wanted a lift!'

The bandits were not like that in Iraq. The first spate of kidnappings of foreigners had just begun, and a World Vision staff member had been killed, so Sheila and her colleagues remained in Jordan, waiting for the situation to improve. Eventually (in 2004) they carried out day trips into Iraq. They would cross over the border from Jordan to meet with Iraqi staff at the police station near the frontier:

We'd intended moving back to our office in Al Rutba, but received a firm warning not to do so. Masked men armed with anti-tank weapons turned up, threatened to blow the place up and warned us not to come back.

Such a warning was taken very seriously. Even the office landlord took his building back, as he didn't want to risk it being blown up. We continued meeting our national team at the border for some time. But finally, following the death of a member of national staff, the decision was taken to close down the programme.

The day trips across the border were 'interesting', she says. They remained alert throughout the journey and were cautious of other vehicles driving alongside them. Forever diligent, their driver would check the vehicle for devices before allowing them to get back in for the return journey.

So what helped to prepare Sheila for this highly unorthodox lifestyle? She was born in Sligo on the north-west coast of Ireland. She grew up with her parents and three brothers. 'Being the only girl was both an advantage and a disadvantage,' she jokes. They lived on a dairy farm, which meant a seven-day working week, 365 days a year. Sheila's father not only milked cows twice a day but also bottled the milk and delivered it door-to-door in their town, morning and night.

Even as young children, the family had their chores to do. Housework, washing milk bottles, filling, capping and crating the bottles, supervising younger siblings when their parents were out on the farm, helping with hay making in the summer, potato picking, fruit picking and jam making were just some of the routine tasks.

The children grew up with a sense of responsibility. They were not afraid of hard work. While they never had a family holiday, the youngsters would go off to children's and youth camps. Sheila explains:

Having some understanding of farm life has helped me to understand and appreciate more the rural communities in countries like Romania, Honduras, Uganda, Afghanistan and so on. It's a good talking point. The price of land and farm animals is always of interest—even types of farm tools and machinery used. The Irish potato is also well known throughout the developing world.

Sheila went to a local 'country' school that had just two teachers. She was a member of a Catholic community with a small group of Protestants. For Religious Education, they had a Catholic priest for four days and a Protestant vicar for one day. Straight after secondary school, she went to a hospital across the road for nursing training. Then she moved to Scotland, where she did midwifery training, and she worked as a midwife on the Isle of Man until the early 1990s. Just after that was when the rollercoaster ride started.

Most recently, Sheila has been working with World Vision Ireland. She has also been finishing a Master's degree in disaster relief health care. So what keeps her going? 'I believe God has called me to do this,' she said. 'It feels right.'

Back to Rwanda. At the end of her time there, they had a feedback session. When team members started sharing what they appreciated about each other, Sheila thought they might say something about her technical expertise:

But what they appreciated was that I always asked if they'd eaten and, if they hadn't, shared my food with them. As many of them had experienced extreme hunger, food was a massive thing to them.

Treating people as valuable and equal is really important. You don't have to be an expert. It's your attitude and behaviour that will be remembered.

Chapter 2

History maker

He hobbled his way down muddy streets, and into the corridors of power. Kujtim Topuzi explains how he became the first young person to address Albania's parliament.

You will stab me in my lips
And I will feel the pain
Because I just would want to tell you
I love you
FROM 'STAB IN THE HEART' BY KUJTIM

Its name is Turkish for 'fortress'. Tucked inside the remains of its ancient city walls is the tomb of a warrior, complete with helmet and arms. Today, Elbasan is the fourth largest town in modern Albania. But heroism has not disappeared from its streets.

Kujtim Topuzi might not fit the usual criteria for a champion. Simple tasks like walking to college are a challenge for this 18-year-old. Yet every day he determinedly edges his way over the bumpy roads on crutches.

He was born with a physical disability in his left leg—but Kujtim walks by faith, and that faith moved him to make a stand for his generation. His clear passion as a campaigner for children's rights made him the perfect candidate to address the Albanian parliament on 1 December 2005, on the occasion of World AIDS Day. He became the first young person to do so:

Today is the International Day Against AIDS and on 3rd of December is the International Day for People with Disability. I am here today to bring the voice and the messages of these two groups of children before you. From the statistics, there are only seven children infected by HIV so far in Albania. Meanwhile, the number of children infected by the virus all over the world reaches 2.5 million—or nearly seven per cent of the entire world infected population.

Maybe in Albania the figures do not present any alarming situation. But it can become like that. Some things need to be improved in the National Strategy for the Prevention and Care of HIV and AIDS in Albania. That's why I am here today, to appeal on behalf of children.

A native of Elbasan, Kujtim and his brother and sister were brought up mainly by their mother Kristina. Their father had to travel to Greece to find work. The family had to make do with a modest income that Dad sent home, with very little assistance from the Albanian government. Despite his disability, Kujtim helped with the household chores and sometimes even babysat his younger siblings.

His homeland—this so-called 'land of the eagles'—was the most restrictive and isolated of Eastern European countries throughout much of the 20th century. It was the last nation to emerge from a strict communist regime in 1991. Since then, this country has struggled through poor leadership and economic collapse to move forward into the future.

As a result, many Albanians are highly sceptical of working together to transform their nation. Most feel that they have been disempowered as a community. However, Kujtim seems to have inherited a determination and resolve from a more ancient time and place. He has a warrior's heart:

I was born with a disability. But as a child I did not feel any different. My family always treated me as anyone else in the household. I grew up believing that I was equal, but oftentimes I am hurt by those who do not think so. My family has been a full support to me. I feel that all those with disabilities should believe that they are equal, just as I was convinced since childhood that I was equal.

Those people should have faith and walk in faith that they, like others, can fight for their rights. I am fully convinced that I am equal because of the way my family has raised me. I do not appreciate it when people feel bad for me, or pity me.

Kujtim's determination and inspirational way of looking at the world have helped him overcome many challenges. Just coping with his environment would be enough for many other people. Elbasan's factories once earned it an unfortunate reputation as one of the most polluted cities in Europe. Most of its roads are either covered with potholes or under construction. When it rains, the streets are muddy.

Amid this grim setting, in one of Europe's poorest nations, Kujtim has looked beyond his own needs to the needs of others. Kujtim is now attending university, but when he was in high school he became president of the student government. There, he started to hear about World Vision. He has since become a popular member of World Vision Albania's educational activities programme. One staff member, Eris, describes him as bright, capable and dependable. 'He is very organized with his work,' she says. 'He likes politics and loves to educate others on children's rights issues.' Clearly, as he explains, his Christian faith has been a key factor behind that:

I grew up with an Orthodox background. As a little child, I was nurtured by the family's tradition. I always liked going to church and respect all the rights and this distinct tradition. At ten years old, I participated in a choir. Later on, I participated in two summer youth camps where I found my faith strengthened.

God is an important part of my life. Faith has helped me in relating to other people because, for me, the main goal of faith is brotherhood. I respect people and expect others to do the same in return. Faith also helps me to set objectives and achieve my goals, knowing that God will help me all through the process.

As an active participant in World Vision activities, it wasn't long before Kujtim drew the attention of the rest of the team. World

Vision Albania and its coalition facilitated a hearing for the country's parliamentary members on health issues. They wanted to raise awareness for the rights of children with HIV and AIDS, and children with disabilities.

Against the backdrop of Albania's social, political and economical unrest has been the issue of behavioural changes, particularly among young people, which have led to a rise in the incidence of Sexually Transmitted Infections (STIs). A study by UNICEF examined the problems encountered by especially vulnerable young people in Albania and their experiences of HIV and AIDS.

The study highlighted a number of factors that make young Albanians particularly vulnerable to the disease. They included high unemployment, a highly mobile population—both internal and travelling abroad for seasonal work—the sudden and recent liberaliz-ation of sexual behaviour, the increase of human trafficking and a weak education system. To tackle all those issues in front of Albania's intimidating government, World Vision needed a champion, and they found one in Kujtim. 'I became a good candidate to speak in front of the parliament,' he recalls. 'I was nervous in the beginning. But in the end I felt honoured.'

The patriarchal and conservative nature of Albanian society has made people extremely hesitant to talk about their beliefs and fears regarding sexual behaviour and the risk of disease. Abuse and violence are other factors, which are a source of shame and are therefore pushed underground. So it is remarkable that someone of Kujtim's age felt brave enough to take such a bold stance on these issues.

In his speech, he raised the plight of children living with HIV and AIDS with the government directly, including a plea to consider their vulnerability regarding AIDS and to take measures to prevent the spread of the disease. He also spoke of the need to strengthen the health services and to protect the physical, psychological and social integrity of youngsters already living with HIV and AIDS throughout Albania. After addressing those issues, Kujtim spoke on behalf of children with disabilities:

We're all different from each other. Some are tall, the others short. Some wear glasses, others do not. Some have coloured skin, others have white. But in front of the so-called 'law', we are equal. Maybe I do not hold your position, but I think I am a part of those children who are in the most appropriate position to raise their voices and bring to your attention the problems children with disabilities face.

Targeting parliamentary members directly, Kujtim thanked them for preparing legislation for those with disabilities. Under the media spotlight, he exposed areas in the legislation that he believed were not nearly strong enough. Reflecting on the experience, he felt it was a privilege to speak about children with disabilities, HIV and AIDS. 'The words came straight from my heart,' he recalls. 'I was filled with emotion, but I was not at all nervous or afraid to address the parliament. I spoke with passion because it is very important for the future of children like me.'

Children and young people like Kujtim receive a modest amount of assistance from their government. Even the simple provision of wheelchair ramps in schools is accomplished through NGOs like World Vision, not the Albanian authorities. Kujtim made sure that he issued a personal request for children with disabilities like himself. 'Please give to children with disabilities the opportunities to integrate in public schools,' he told politicians. 'Please stop discrimination towards these children.'

Parliamentary members responded by promising to send a letter with instructions and recommendations to the Ministry of Health. World Vision Albania's National Director Nicholas Gummere was impressed by Kujtim's performance. 'As a highly capable person with a disability, Kujtim can speak better than me on the risks and concerns of vulnerable children in Albania,' he says. He believes that having someone such as Kujtim speak at such a high-level hearing is exactly how it should be. 'Principle 4 of the United Nations Convention on the Rights of the Child provides that children should be involved in decisions that affect them.'

Kujtim is involved in campaigning at other levels, too. He is in contact with local organizations for people with disabilities, and tries to make a stand wherever he goes:

Personally, if any of my friends make nasty comments about people with disabilities, I will try to talk to them and make them aware that all people are equal. I try to do as opportunities arise. I also believe that good campaigns can only come from people with disabilities themselves. People with disabilities need to be invited in to make decisions concerning issues affecting them.

Away from the campaigning, Kujtim gets to grips with the demands of home life and a full schedule of studies at university. Home is a three-bedroom house, where he used to have to share a room with his brother. 'It's not the most comfortable house,' he says. 'I wish I could have my own room and I would like to have a computer in my room as well. We have a small garden with some fruit trees.' Two cats and some chickens complete the household.

He has to take a bus to the city centre. From there, he walks to university. He spends most of his time there, and sometimes, after lectures, he attends extra-curricular courses like computing, English and Italian. When he's not at those lessons, Kujtim can be found at the local Internet café, doing some research before returning home. There's that determination again—he wants to make a difference:

In the future I want to write for a good newspaper where I can express my opinions freely. Also, I see no reason why I cannot become an honest politician. My dream is that one day there will be a world where everyone is independent from their physical and mental limits, and they feel equal with all the others. Keeping in mind that I will graduate with a journalist degree and maybe will end up working in TV or newspaper, I want to write and sensitize the government and major organizations about issues that will bring up a healthy generation.

I want to write articles for young people showing what a healthy life is, a life without drugs and alcohol. I also want to promote activities that young people can be involved in, to get themselves away from bad habits. I want to establish a youth centre in a village, then young people can come together to discuss.

Spoken like a real politician!

✢

Chapter 3

New morning

Civil war wrecked her homeland for nearly two decades, but now Zoubeida is helping a new generation to make a fresh start in Lebanon's beautiful Bekaa valley.

Praying as we work can produce calm amid chaos. (Anon)

A new day dawns over Lebanon, and people like Zoubeida Amine Abou Assaly are doing what they can to rebuild their nation. As leader of a World Vision programme, she is helping to project a different future for her people.

At 23, Zoubeida is far too young to recall the conflict that ripped her nation apart from 1976 to 1991. But older friends and relatives have related their own experiences of that horrific war that claimed tens of thousands of lives, and they involved Zoubeida from an early age:

My parents told me that when I was one year old, they started to hear the bombs coming closer to our house. So they didn't know what to do, and waited for my father to come home. When my father came, he told us that it was not safe to go outside, so he took us all to a small room to hide inside.

The minute that we entered, a bomb fell at our house. But by the grace of God nothing happened to any one of us. My parents carried me and my two-year-old brother to the shelter that's a bit far from us, and stayed for a long time there.

The war was played out on TV news clips across the globe. But as Westerners watched from the comfort of their suburban homes, the reality was that more than 100,000 people were killed and another 100,000 injured during those unrelenting battles.

About 900,000 people—up to one-fifth of the pre-war population—were displaced from their homes. About a quarter of a million of them emigrated permanently. Thousands of people lost limbs as a result of the planting of landmines. The fighting split the capital Beirut across the so-called 'Green Line'. That once-glorious city was divided between the Christian-dominated east and the Muslim west. Central government all but broke down, despite attempts to find a political solution.

Since those days of devastation, however, relative calm has been returning, as Zoubeida explains:

The people of Zahle suffered a lot from the war: they lost their homes, jobs and family members. The older generation has had lots of problems and sufferings. It was hard for them to build their future and find work, because the war destroyed everything. But the present generation is much better… all of them are working together to rebuild Lebanon.

Lebanon's new morning is just as dependent on grassroots activity as on high-level political talks. That process includes people like Zoubeida, quietly getting on with rewriting their nation's story behind the headlines and well away from the spotlight of the world's media. She is currently working as co-ordinator of a World Vision project called Kids' Kingdom.

The idea behind this scheme is simple: set up a centre that is free of charge for all, but which will make every child who steps inside feel as if he or she is living as a king or queen in his or her kingdom. The goal has always been to offer hope to poor children aged 4–16, who have never played with proper toys and have never even heard the centuries-old story about Jesus.

The project is based in Zoubeida's home town, Zahle, an area known as the 'Bride of the Bekaa' because of its attractive setting.

Predominantly Christian, this red-roofed town nestles amid dramatic mountain scenery. The first sight that visitors often see is a statue celebrating wine and culture, because Zahle styles itself as 'The City of Wine and Poetry'. Zoubeida describes it:

All the way to the end of the city, the Berdauni river separates the main street into two, decorating the roadsides with green trees, and flowing all the way outside Zahle. From its hills, you can see fields of different colours, as if a carpet has been laid... Green mountains covered with red and yellow flowers can be seen in the spring.

You can smell the soil when it begins to rain. And what a wonderful feeling you get when walking next to the river on the fallen yellow and orange leaves that are spread all over the sidewalk! Summer is not too hot, but the best view is when sitting on your balcony and watching the sun as it slides from behind Zahle's mountains to rest.

Kids' Kingdom is located right there, amid history and beauty—on a street that separates Christians from Muslims. Creative and educational activities are held in a suite of brightly lit, child-friendly rooms on the first floor of an apartment block. Most of the walls are decorated with paintings and drawings by the children who attend the programme.

The library room is the largest. This remarkable resource boasts encyclopedias, dictionaries and books in English, French and Arabic, offering a treasury of material. There is also a big video screen, puzzles, musical instruments and toys. Of course, the screen is in constant use!

In addition, there are two toy rooms (popular with all the youngsters), a computer room offering nine terminals, and a craft room, where the children can draw, paint or do any sort of handicraft they like. A kitchen is used to teach them how to cook. Zoubeida had never seen anything like it:

When I first saw it, I was impressed. The words weren't enough to tell what was in my heart. I'd never seen a centre for kids with such values, that welcomes all kids for free and, above all, teaches them about Jesus. That was the first time I heard about World Vision, and it made me very proud of being a volunteer with them.

It has been an interesting journey for Zoubeida. Brought up in a Christian household, she decided to follow Jesus for herself when she was just nine. The location was a children's camp run by the evangelical churches in the Bekaa valley. 'It was very exciting,' she recalls, 'because I had never been in such a camp and seen such programmes and games.'

Sunday school and youth meetings helped her to grow in her faith, but she credits World Vision as being the biggest inspiration. 'I learned how to depend completely on God in everything I do,' she says. 'I learned that I could do nothing right except through Jesus.'

For her main education, Zoubeida attended an evangelical school. She was taught about the Bible and took part in devotions. Classes were run by missionaries from England, Holland and the USA. The sacrifices they had made left a lasting impression on Zoubeida:

One family came all the way from England to serve the Lord at our school. They came with their children, too. It happened by chance that they lived in the same building that I do.

They left a very big influence in my heart and life. I learned from them how to put all my problems on the cross. I saw the very nice way they lived, and how they dealt with people. This made me thirsty to drink more from the word of God.'

Such experiences, coupled with the fact that she lived in such a shattered land, caused Zoubeida to dream. She dreamt of becoming a missionary, of bringing hope to others. At 14 she was already teaching in Sunday school. 'I had a yearning in my heart,' she remembers. That feeling grew stronger as the years passed. 'I couldn't wait to get bigger to achieve my aim,' she says. A simple line from Sunday school kept urging her on. It was the New Testament call to 'go into all the world and preach the good news to all creation' (Mark 16:15).

I felt that this was from God to me, because every time I hear about famine or poor people or any natural disaster, this verse comes into my mind. I had that feeling from a young age—and I wanted to achieve my goal and serve people.

On leaving school, Zoubeida considered moving to the USA to study there. Her brother had just done that very thing. She applied and was accepted. Her next step was to obtain a visa, but something stopped her in her tracks:

I woke up one morning and saw my mother crying and praying that God wouldn't let me go. I deleted all my traveling plans… I got a phone call the next day and was asked to volunteer at a centre opened by World Vision.

She started working there, alongside the staff, and began to feel as if her dreams were coming true. All her life, Zoubeida had wanted to work with the poor and oppressed—especially children. Now here she was, doing that very thing, in her own town.

After three months, she was chosen from among many to join the salaried staff. Without giving her a formal interview, the World Vision team virtually handed her the job. 'I didn't refuse,' she says. 'I thought it was a blessing from God.'

Zoubeida thought that was a challenge, but then along came another. After just six months of serving at the centre, Zoubeida became the manager. 'I went to bed one night as an assistant, and woke up the next morning as co-ordinator' is how she remembers it:

I was just a 20-year-old university girl, managing a centre of 300 kids with no assistants, all by myself, preparing programmes, sitting and talking with the kids, dealing with parents, administrative matters and dealing with a few volunteers.

I used to do all these daily with my studies at university, courses and

*training at work… but since it was for God's service, it was bearable.
I didn't count the hours I spent at work, because I wanted to give the
best results to my managers, World Vision and Jesus, too. And through
complete dependence on him, I overcame it.*

These days, she has plenty of help. She has a full-time assistant and
five volunteer helpers. In addition, there are more than eight women
who lend a hand whenever they bring their children to the centre.
Interestingly, women from different faiths like to volunteer at the
centre, too.

Children usually arrive at 4pm, after finishing school for the
day. First of all, they have some free time to play in the toy room,
computer room or library. Stories are told, songs are sung and
handicrafts are made. The centre staff do this for 200 children every
month.

Working to improve the body, mind and spirit of all kinds of
youngsters—of all religions and ages—are the highlights of Zoubeida's work. 'You won't find any organization in Lebanon that
works in all of those areas for the kids,' she says. But it's not without
incident.

One day, the sound of an explosion ripped through the building.
It was like an echo from Zoubeida's past, but when she investigated,
all she found was a fog of dust and powder. It turned out that eight-
year-old Joe had been messing with the fire extinguisher! With just
half an hour before the parents would arrive, Zoubeida could have
lost it and just shouted at the children. She prayed instead. Joe was
trembling in the corner of the room, tears rolling down his cheeks.
Zoubeida hugged him until his mother showed up.

Early the next day, Joe's mother was waiting at the gate. This
time it was Zoubeida who was trembling, but she mustered up the
courage to chat with her. She discovered that the boy hadn't stopped
crying even after returning home—but not because of the fire
extinguisher.

'You and Dad always shout at me when I do wrong,' he'd told
his parents, 'and you're always too busy to hug and love me. Our

teachers at Kids' Kingdom are so different. Even when I've done wrong and they have the right to shout at me, I find love, understanding and patience that I never find at home. I wish I was born at Kids' Kingdom!'

Joe's mother cried as she talked. 'I'd like to change my approach with my family and find peace in my life,' she admitted, 'but I don't know how!' The two women spent the morning talking about parenthood and faith.

A few days later, Joe's mum returned to say, 'Now I'm feeling the real meaning of peace.'

Kids' Kingdom was closed during the worst of the conflict in 2006, but reopened in September and continues its vital work.

✝

Chapter 4

One peace at a time

It's been described as 'the most dramatic race against the clock', but Ayalew Teshome has been clawing back time for the people of Southern Sudan.

The effects of flood, drought, famine, an abortive defection attempt, and a major disagreement with local leaders, are just some of the challenges that faced Ayalew Teshome after he started work with World Vision. Yet he has managed not only to survive, but also to thrive in serving the needy people of Southern Sudan, for Ayalew is not actually regarded as a staff member of a relief agency. He is accepted as a brother and respected as an elder.

Currently Field Operations Director of the Southern Sudan programme, Ayalew joined the organization at a critical time in 1998. Four emergency response projects had been underway in Tonj, the key area of operations. 'The region was hit by two natural calamities —flood and drought—for two consecutive seasons,' he explains. 'That caused crop failure and exposed the entire community to one of the worst famines in the country's history.'

An abortive defection attempt by a prominent militia leader had led to a huge displacement of communities who had decided to flee for safety. There had also been disagreements between World Vision and local leaders, so the project in Tonj county was suspended. All international staff members were pulled out, souring relationships with community leaders. To top it all, the government had banned humanitarian flights. 'My task was to provide humanitarian service to the needy Sudanese amid all these challenges,' Ayalew recalls.

It is critical that key staff are acceptable not only to World Vision but also to the local community. The community can reject a person they dislike for whatever reason. Ayalew was recruited into that context.

Fortunately, the community liked him. The relationship with World Vision was restored and the projects restarted. That risky initiation has since marked his time there, and has helped resolve one conflict after another. As Ayalew explains, 'I was able to engage in dialogue with the leaders and re-establish good relationship. I convinced World Vision management to continue serving the community—and the project grew both in type and size.'

So what is his secret? Ayalew does not presume to have the full answer, but he can point to some factors that have worked in his favour:

Although I was passionate and committed, I was unshakeable when it came to issues that would compromise principles. I think they have tested me and proven that I was doing the right thing.

I take time to listen to their problems and their views before I make a decision. They have known me for being firm in my decisions and principles. I guess these could be some of the reasons for the trust in me.

Ayalew was born in 1953 in Wollo, Ethiopia, 800 kilometres north of the capital, Addis Ababa. Ethiopia has been a refuge for many southern Sudanese who fled their country—another reason for the respect shown by locals to Ayalew.

Wollo is part of the Great Rift Valley, site of some of the earliest human settlements. It is also where the 1974 famine took more than 100,000 lives, triggering a political crisis that ended the reign of Emperor Haile Selassie.

When Ayalew was just three, his father was killed by bandits. So it was left to his mother, helped by some of his uncles, to bring him up. 'They saw me as very precious and took care of me as a special child,' he says. Unusually, his uncles told him not to climb trees or play in the fields, but to watch local court cases and see how situations were resolved. Through that experience, he was already being prepared for his future destiny.

Most of his schooling took place around the village where he was raised. Education was mainly the responsibility of local Orthodox churches. Nine-year-old Ayalew learned about religion and how to read and write Amharic.

A year later, he ran away from school with four older boys from his village. They walked for more than ten days, in search of a better education.

On the third day of our journey we met some people from our village who were coming from Addis Ababa where we were heading, who tried to convince us to go back home.

Of course, since we were determined, we refused. But they went with the good news to our families back home, telling them where they had met us and informing them where we were heading.

When their families received the information, they made a number of attempts to take the boys back, but none of their efforts was fruitful. Ayalew was adamant and determined to continue with his education. In the end, his family felt they had to leave him alone to carry on with what he wanted to do. The young Ayalew had to lead an independent life with minimal financial support—in fact, barely enough for his clothing.

Normally, children run away from school, not to school. Not Ayalew! On reflection, he believes he made such a radical move because his late father mentioned plans for him to get a good education.

In 1964 Ayalew met two female students from an evangelical college. They inspired him and even committed themselves to paying towards school fees and books, if Ayalew could get assistance for his food and accommodation. About a year later, he was able to get a weekend job. In 1965, he enrolled in a school. He completed his first three years of primary education in one year. Eventually, he scored 99.6 per cent in national examination results.

Ayalew went on to complete his secondary education. But his formal schooling was disrupted by student uprisings over demands for democratic rights, so he decided to train as an engineer with the Ethiopian Air Force. After completing two years of engineering training, he started his working life with the Air Force in 1973 as an aircraft mechanic. He also worked as an internal auditor and editor of the *Ethiopian Air Force Review*.

The Air Force has a special place in my history… I was one of three top performing trainees who have the privilege to choose a career from the range of technical departments.

I served for the first couple of years as a jet engine technician, maintaining and servicing the US-made F-86 and F-5 jet engines at the depot level, and later as a technician on Soviet-made Mig aircraft.

During this time, Ayalew married and started a family. In 1986, he was transferred to the Ministry of National Defence to assume new responsibilities until 1991—but dramatic changes had already begun around him.

Ayalew had been born into the feudal system headed by Haile Selassie. This ancient monarchical state was going through major political changes. Communism had replaced capitalism. An age-old empire with Judeo-Christian roots had become crippled by restrictions on worship and religious practice. Power struggles between political factions resulted in bloodshed.

'A number of my colleagues perished in the process,' Ayalew remembers. Continuing changes in the system, coupled with political instability and insecurity, forced him to consider his future. He discussed the options with his wife, Snafkish Desta. They agreed that he should not fall into the hands of the Ethiopian Peoples Democratic revolutionary forces. He should escape. 'I had to flee my country, leaving my family behind, and restart from scratch in Kenya,' says Ayalew. 'This was a very bitter decision. But we thought the other options would be worse.'

He left Ethiopia just a few days before forces took control of

Addis Ababa and seized power in May 1991. Those who decided to stay were detained. Some have since been released, but they continue to find life difficult.

Ayalew recalls that, for him, the first two years in exile were the hardest. Back home, his wife was subjected to frequent interrogations by the authorities. She even had her salary stopped.

Those three years were the loneliest time of my life. How my lovely wife managed on her own, I still don't know. But I am truly grateful. Glory be to the Lord, who gave her the perseverance to take care of our children.

Despite being lonely, separated from my family, it was in Kenya that my Christian life has been restored and I began serving God's people, the Sudanese.

He returned to school to do a postgraduate diploma course in business management at Kenya Institute of Management. He joined the humanitarian industry in 1993 in Southern Sudan, with a German organization. The family was finally reunited in Nairobi in 1994.

In 1997 Ayalew began to work in northern Uganda as a construction engineer in Sudanese refugee camps—'a job that fulfilled my desire of serving needy people'. The next year, he saw an advert in the Kenyan *Daily Nation* newspaper.

World Vision was looking for a manager for one of their sites in Sudan, a country split between the largely Christian community in the south and the predominantly Muslim north. Since 1983, at least two million had died in fighting or famine. World Vision had been operating there since the 1970s.

Ayalew applied for the job. He felt he fulfilled the requirements but was called only after the other candidates were disqualified. 'I was called, interviewed and duly informed that I had been successful,' he remembers. So what were his first impressions? 'Although my salary package was slightly lower than what I had been getting from my previous employer, joining World Vision was a real fulfilment for me —where I could serve needy people and nurture my Christian life.'

On joining in 1998, his first job was as project manager for one of the two sites in Southern Sudan, at Bahr el Ghazal. Later, he became Sudan Operation Advisor, before joining the management team as Field Operations Director.

It is a massive challenge to work in a place with hardly any national infrastructure. Most of Southern Sudan has no running water, roads, electricity or phone services. Ayalew hopes he will see that change:

Because of my background, my ambitions, hope and dreams have always been geared towards helping people who are in need, and doing things that help people come out of their problems.

I have scraped through life. I have had it rough, very rough at times. Running away from home and scavenging to survive to the next day was an experience that made me want to help others in need.

His resilience and understanding helped him negotiate the release of three World Vision workers who were taken hostage in 2003. Ekkehard Forberg, Steffen Horstmeier and Andrew Omwenga had been abducted during a militia attack in Waat. A fourth employee, Charles Kibbe, was killed.

Rebel forces deeply regretted the death. In a statement they recognized the role of relief workers in administering aid for the people of Southern Sudan. Ayalew has other stories from his involvement in the region:

While supervising non-food items distribution, I came across a young lady, aged about 19, carrying a three-year-old child covered with a piece of cloth. She was seeking support like everyone else.

She looked desperate. Through an interpreter, I asked about her child. The child had actually died the day before. She was carrying the body around because there was no one to help her to bury him.

Such accounts are commonplace in this broken land. According to a United Nations official, the Sudan crisis 'is the most dramatic race against the clock anywhere in the world at the moment'.

Ayalew and his team have made inroads. In 2005, at Thiet, Ngabagog, Luonyaker and Panacier Therapeutic Feeding Centres in war-torn Tonj and Gogrial counties, thousands of children were saved from severe malnutrition through a food aid programme aimed at under-fives.

Food aid not only sustains the children. It also allows their parents to hope. In recent times a measure of peace has come to this troubled nation. Ayalew feels fulfilled. 'We're making progress,' he says, and continues:

When I started working there, we were paying people in second-hand clothes, salt and soap. That was the level they were at. Now the country is developing and getting more exposure.

As the peace continues to hold, the desire to develop the country is growing very fast… I want to see Sudan become part of the world. The journey has begun.

Ayalew remains key to the effort there. He has earned the confidence of both World Vision and the local community. The present government of Southern Sudan consider him a friend.

His personal involvement is still costly: the job keeps him away from home and doesn't allow for weekends or leave. Yet his 19-year-old daughter Addis-hiwot Ayalew and 17-year-old son Abiy Ayalew continue to be supportive. At the same time, like all children, they can be very honest and challenging with their comments.

Sooner or later, every parent has to face one or two home truths from their children. Ayalew says, 'My daughter recently looked at me and jokingly asked, "Dad, when will you stop living for the Sudanese and start living for yourself?"'

The situation in Sudan is constantly changing, but updates may be found at the website www.alertnet.org.

Chapter 5

Place of miracles

There are signs of hope in Colombia—the children and young people who fight for peace. Mayerly Sanchez is one of them.

It has been called the most dangerous place in the Western hemisphere. Yet, from the streets of Bogotá emerged a World Vision sponsored child who helped lead millions in a massive peace movement. Mayerly Sanchez is one of the 'peace soldiers' of Colombia.

Most people could describe their own town or city as a place of contrasts, but in Bogotá this is true on a grand scale. High-rise buildings dwarf colonial churches. Spanish-style streets lie close to shanty towns. Businessmen walk the same roads as crippled beggars, gypsy performers, terrorists and drug dealers.

This larger-than-life drama is played out against a stunning mountain backdrop. As if nature reflects Colombian culture, the landscape is captivating but cruel. The mountains form a portal for some terrifying storms. Thunder, lightning and rain sweep past the peaks and strike the cosmopolitan heartland.

On the ground below, the mortal clash is between government forces, leftist guerillas, paramilitary death squads and wealthy drug lords. Murder, kidnapping, torture and displacement are all a part of daily life in Colombia.

Mayerly was born amid this chaos in 1984. She lived with her mother, father and older sister in the slums of Soacha. This marginal area on the outskirts of Bogotá had become home for displaced families and the poorest people of the city. Some made their homes in shelters of plastic and cardboard.

Most of the inhabitants didn't have the resources or appropriate materials to build housing. There were no public services such as clean water and a sewage system, so people had to walk for hours to get water—and, with unpaved roads, that wasn't an easy trek. Mayerly remembers:

We were living in my grandparents' house, because we could not afford to rent our own place. Our economic situation was hard. We used to live on the salary of my father.

I undertook primary education at a public school near my house. When I was eight, World Vision started to work in my community. I was one of those chosen to be affiliated to the sponsorship programme, along with my older sister.

When she was in fourth grade, Mayerly started attending the Timothy Club, a place where children could get together for recreation every Saturday. Some months later, the club leader moved to another part of the city.

Acting on their own initiative, Mayerly and her friends decided to organize their own activities, in a bid to offer children alternative ways of spending their free time. It wasn't about just giving them something to do. It was about throwing them a lifeline amid the violence and poverty, as Mayerly explains:

In my neighbourhood, poverty is reflected in each one of the homes. Most of the families live on less than a dollar a day, and education—though it's a right and should be provided by the government—is not offered to all the children.

Parents have to look for an income doing whatever is possible and leaving their children at home the whole day. This is an opportunity for people with evil intentions to try to involve children in drugs, alcoholism, armed groups and activities that generate even more violence and delinquency.

The human debris haunted her. Even some of her own friends were killed, having done nothing wrong in their short lives. They became tiny statistics in Colombia's 50-year-long internal struggle, as armed factions have sought to wipe out the government. Mayerly was confounded. She asked herself, 'What can we do?'

She and her friends started to look for more alternatives to the deep unrest and bitter conflict that they saw around them. They realized that they could bring young people together under the banner of sports, so they organized soccer and basketball competitions. Many children became involved.

These youngsters started to see that respect could be earned through sporting prowess rather than being demanded down the barrel of a gun. Mayerly and her comrades recognized that education is empowerment. So, with the support of World Vision, they received training on children's rights and duties:

We were chosen to be part of the Peace Builders Movement because of the work we were doing in our community. We became responsible for teaching local children all that we were learning. By that time, I had started secondary education and was attending a public school, one hour's walk from my house.

The Peace Builders Movement came about in 1996. UNICEF brought together all the institutions working with children in Colombia to focus on children's rights. The new alliance aimed to increase understanding of the impact of war on children. Each group had to appoint a representative. Mayerly was chosen by youngsters from her community and by children affiliated to World Vision to represent them.

One of the first acts of the movement was to mobilize children to vote in a special election, the Children's Mandate for Peace and Rights. It was a brave move. A group toured schools and churches and had talks with children about their rights, while also emphasizing their responsibilities. Youngsters were asked to choose which of their rights were most important to them and their communities. World Vision played an active part in the programme.

Initially, it was expected that about 300,000 children would cast their vote. However, the movement took off, and nearly three million people aged 7–18 turned out at the polls. They voted overwhelmingly in favour of the right to survival and the right to peace.

These young people became the driving force behind a national peace movement that continued to gather strength. In 1997, over ten million adult Colombians supported a peace referendum that included backing for the Children's Mandate, condemnation of the atrocities of war and a personal pledge to help make peace. Peace became a top priority in Colombia's political process. It became the primary issue in the presidential elections of 1998 and led to peace talks between the government and guerilla organizations.

Today, more than 100,000 children are active participants in the peace movement. They include children who help other youngsters overcome the trauma of exposure to violence, avoid accidents with landmines and learn how to resolve conflicts. Children also speak to their parents, classmates, teachers, local government officials, the police, the media—and even the President—about making peace. As Mayerly says:

The movement allows children and young people to express their ideas and dreams. The whole aim of our work has been to make more children know about the different problems and their possible solutions. The experience has changed my life, my family and many other children's lives.

After the national vote, Mayerly continued giving talks in schools. She took part in a review of the country's Child Code to campaign against children being forced to serve in paramilitary groups. She participated in major summits and conferences on an international level.

Mayerly scooped third prize in the 2001 World Children's Prize and travelled to Sweden to receive the award from Queen Silvia. She addressed the United Nations in New York at a Special Session on Children. She spoke at the First International Women's Day Observance of the New Millennium. To top it all, Colombia's peace movement was nominated twice for the Nobel Peace Prize.

It's a staggering list of achievements for one young girl and her mates. But the bright lights and summit speeches were over-shadowed a few years ago by the tragic death of Mayerly's father. He died in a workplace incident involving a cement truck. To this day, no compensation has been offered to the family. Mayerly remembers:

It was a difficult time because he was the most important person to us. I was 19, and I became responsible for my mother and my sisters. I started to work part time with World Vision and at the same time I continued studying to be a journalist.

Mayerly had started her professional studies thanks to support from World Vision and CNN. The US-based TV news network took an interest in helping her after featuring her story in a film called *Soldiers of Peace*. The programme showed how these young people risked their lives to bring change.

The aims of the video were to help students explain the causes and effects of the years of violence in Colombia, identify the social, political and economic problems that continue to foster violence there, and analyse why young people have been willing to risk their own safety to promote peace.

Not surprisingly, then, Mayerly continues to pursue her studies into Social Communications, with an emphasis on journalism. Her aim is to uncover the 'hidden history' of her country—from ordinary people who have worked hard behind the scenes to bring about transformation in their land:

I would like to tell their stories, to learn from them, to help those whose voices are not heard to be known, listened to and taken into account. I want to show the Colombians that there are many others doing great things for our country.

I want to be a journalist all my life, a good journalist. I think the most important thing is to love what you do, and I love my profession and I want to use it to help other needy people in the way they did for me.

Her involvement in the peace movement has clearly left her with a striking maturity. As she has said, peace can be defined in four words: love, acceptance, forgiveness and work. Amazingly, she is optimistic—partly because she sees hope in the eyes of the children around her, despite the impossible situations they and their families are going through. Amid all the struggles, they still find the strength and the courage to share a smile. 'They encourage my work,' says Mayerly. 'That is why I have a lifetime commitment.'

Her own personal faith upholds her, too. She adds:

It is a daily journey where each one of the actions that my family and I perform are commended to God. We think that we are tools of his peace. He is the one giving us strength and shelter, supporting and taking care of us at every time.

He has not allowed us to faint in the most difficult times of our lives.

Those who visit Mayerly's city of contrasts are encouraged to take a cable car ride to the top of its highest peak. The Cerro de Montserrat rises to 10,000 feet. It is a favourite with the locals, who go there for the view, the park, the bullring, restaurants—and a religious site.

Here is a church that boasts the statue of Señor Caído, the 'Fallen Christ'. It is an important place of pilgrimage that is also said to be a place of miracles—and, for those who don't like cable cars, it can be reached by climbing hundreds of stairs.

Mayerly and others like her are hoping and praying that Bogotá—and indeed the whole of Colombia—will become a place of miracles. But for now, it might be a bit of a climb before they reach those kinds of spectacular sights.

Chapter 6

Out of the 'sacred house'

Rudo Kwaramba has championed the cause of women in
modern-day Zimbabwe. Now she is a spokesperson
for all those in need.

Would you buy a sixty-quid wedding dress from Asda? That was the
question being put to listeners on a daytime radio programme. The
show's special guest was asked for her opinion. 'Yes, I would,' said
Rudo Kwaramba.

She shared her views during National Marriage Week 2006, an
annual event that raises the profile of traditional marriage in the UK.
As Director of Advocacy, Communication and Education at World
Vision UK, Rudo was looking at some of the hot issues from the
day's news stories.

'The issue is being practical about what you can afford,' she told
listeners of *Woman To Woman*, a programme on London's Premier
Radio. She continued:

*The danger is, when you don't have the option, you kind of find yourself
in a situation where you do want to have a wedding, but the cost is
prohibitive.*

*I think you have to put value on the right things around a wedding. It's
about bringing people together. It's about celebrating something beautiful.
And if having a cheaper wedding gown makes it easier, I would vote for it.*

It was an entertaining discussion that drew a lively response from
the listeners. But the chat around the story about Asda's budget

wedding dress also drew from the deeper well of Rudo's personal beliefs and experiences: 'When you wear it, you bring the uniqueness of who you are. It's up to you to be the person that you are throughout your wedding—and into your marriage.'

Rudo is not a bridal consultant—but she has rubbed shoulders with celebrities. She has shared the same bill as singer-songwriter Billy Bragg, pop star Daniel Bedingfield, actor Pete Postlethwaite and reggae artist Ben Okafor. That was when she was taking part in the Make Poverty History rally in 2005. She was among hundreds of thousands of campaigners who converged on Edinburgh. They sent a clear message to the leaders of the world's richest nations to drop the debt, deliver trade justice and provide more aid.

Rudo is fast becoming a regular media figure. She has addressed subjects close to her heart at the Greenbelt arts festival and the Conservative Christian Fellowship. She has written key articles for publications like *The Guardian* and narrated an African TV series about women and violence. The 13-part series was the first of its kind in Rudo's homeland of Zimbabwe. Stories were told about women from around the country who had suffered abuse. Children had been raped and mothers beaten. The programmes provoked much discussion around the issue, and raised awareness.

Rudo grew up in what she describes as a 'middle-class working family' in Zimbabwe—middle-class in terms of education rather than money. Her parents were both teachers within a rural Dutch Reformed Church Mission.

It was a sheltered but good life. I got the best of both worlds—things like electricity, water and schooling that many other Zimbabweans didn't—but also the feeling of being part of a community.

Life in rural areas was, and still is for many people, hard. But I was spared much of this hardship. Where we lived wasn't luxurious, but it was comfy enough for the white people!

She was the youngest of three children, and the only girl. They were teenagers in 1980 when they moved to the city for her father's new job, working for the Ministry of Education. That same year, after prolonged political conflict with its colonial power Britain, and guerrilla warfare within its own borders, Zimbabwe gained independence (in Bantu, *Zimbabwe* means 'sacred house' or 'ritual seat of a king').

Multiracial schools had been emerging, and Rudo went to one of them. She enjoyed the good education, sporting facilities and so on that this institution had to offer:

We had been living in what was a 'gentler' form of apartheid. But after independence, Zimbabweans had access to better living conditions, a bigger choice of restaurants, shops, etc. There was a gradual feeling of equality that came in, rather than a decree that took effect over night.

High school was a good experience. There were many opportunities in drama, sport and studies. Rudo and her brothers joined the 'right teams' so they could go on the most field trips. According to her, it was a way of 'broadening their horizons'!

Rudo adopted the Christian faith when she was quite young, probably due to the 'mission' upbringing she received. She read the Bible in her own language, Shona, and has a high regard for Bible translators as a result.

In her view, Christianity was one good thing to come out of colonization. Baptism and confirmation were landmarks in her life. Scripture Union camps happened every August, and they helped Rudo to grow in her faith as a teenager. She comments: 'They were fantastic, giving me and my friends a good grounding in the Bible and reading it, the opportunity to escape again from small town life—and a good place to meet nice boys!'

Rudo claims that she did not have much political awareness as a youngster. She lived in a town with 'nice' people. They were grateful for their new privileges. They did not ask many questions. After all, the transition to independence appeared to be going well and things seemed to be changing for the better. But Rudo began to wonder.

When her school swapped its white headmaster for a black

headmaster, she resented that. It felt as if there would be a drop in standards. There was an attitude of 'changing things for the sake of it'—to jettison colonization. Rudo believes that sometimes this led to 'losing the baby with the bath water'.

In 1988 she went to the University of Zimbabwe in Harare to study law. It was not out of a great sense of vocation. Her older brother had wanted to do law, but lacked the grades. 'I'll do law for you,' Rudo said, and she did!

She had a taste of big city life in Harare—quite different from her home town. She felt like 'a small town girl in a new world', and at times it was very challenging, to say the least. Rudo stayed on in the city after graduating and moved into a YMCA hostel for young female workers. After a while, she acquired her own apartment in the city and settled into the local Baptist church:

My reformed background had a lot of rules, so I felt a bit freer to be myself in the Baptist church. I was baptized by immersion after graduating, and it was during this time that I met my husband-to-be.

I now knew snippets of what I wanted to do and where I wanted to go. After studying law, my sense of justice and injustice was heightened. I felt strongly that law that was imposed on people was not real law. Law is not real law until people live it.

Rudo believed that law should be close enough to be relevant to individual lives, but distant enough to be universal. For example, there were two marriage laws in Zimbabwe: one enabled men to be polygamous, the other encouraged them to be monogamous. Both pieces of legislation had an effect on women. No woman wants to share her husband, but customs meant that some women had to and were therefore vulnerable to difficult marriages. Rudo's passion for women and justice began to form:

I practised law for one year after university. Ever the drama lover, I wanted the chance to go before a judge in a gown and wig—and enjoyed the power to liberate, to change and empower someone else.

People's lives can be changed for the better. I could now use my knowledge for the good of people who may otherwise have been powerless.

While between jobs, Rudo stumbled across an organization working with women. She volunteered to help abused women, assisting them with protection orders and child support. She found that the law was not enough. She developed a passion for helping women, especially those affected by violence. Then she was offered another job for a prestigious, white law firm. Much to her brother's annoyance, she could not take it: she stayed with the women's rights organization, and never regretted her decision.

Women were looked down on in Zimbabwe. Rudo's interest and concern were partly fuelled by the fact that occasionally her father had been violent towards her mother:

I enjoyed helping to empower women about their own identity. Part of this liberation came through faith—and faith brings confidence. Often it wasn't appropriate for me to preach, but I would point to God as a way of repairing a shattered self-esteem.

I felt equipped to do this job through my understanding of law, and stayed for five years. I was also involved in the national women's human rights movement that was pushing for constitutional change.

Progress was made. But Rudo fears that in modern-day Zimbabwe, the situation for women has gone from bad to worse. She claims that in the 2000 election, many women were violated yet received no help. Police were too busy responding to the needs of the white farmers and others with influence.

Rudo started working for the United Nations High Commission for Refugees as a Protection Officer. She was working with refugees from Burundi, Rwanda, Sudan, Somalia and Eastern Europe who were living in transit camps. She stayed there for a year. The director of the NGO for whom she used to work left, and she took on that role.

During this time she was invited to become a council member for World Vision Zimbabwe, which was looking for a female lawyer. She enjoyed this role but found it 'strange' how World Vision worked. In her eyes, it was focused on development and some relief, but did not engage much with human rights. Although concerned that World Vision 'wasn't activist enough', she accepted the invitation to become its new director.

I was still a bit frustrated. Previously, the human rights movement wasn't especially relevant to the poorest people. Now my work was with the poorest people, but didn't involve human rights. I wanted to join it all up together.

My five years there were a lot of hard work, but also very fulfilling. I appreciated the fact that, although World Vision is international, it works hard to be 'local'. It also lives out its Christian values.

One day, Rudo was visiting a food distribution point in Gwanda, a key farming and mining town. People lined up in seemingly endless queues, waiting for food. The queues consisted mainly of old women, because many of the young were sick or dead. Zimbabwe was being crippled by AIDS. As one of the old women approached the front of the queue, she exclaimed, 'Surely, there is a God in heaven.' She recognized God in the response to the food crisis. Rudo was inspired and encouraged by this reaction.

After five years as national director in Zimbabwe, the political pressure on Rudo was growing. She had little time to spend with her husband Alexander and son Isheanesu Joshua. So she sought opportunities elsewhere:

Canada seemed appealing. It was somewhere in between the USA, which was 'loud', and the UK, which was 'snobbish'! However, I met the chief executive of World Vision UK, and he told me about possible roles open there.

I was offered a job. Although I wasn't sure, I was swayed by a World Vision colleague from Africa who said, 'If a young girl is of marriageable age and keeps turning down suitors, she might end up unmarried… give the English a chance!' So I did.

That move, of course, has led to her representing World Vision at some high-profile events, which brings us back to the Premier Radio broadcast. During her guest slot, Rudo reflected on the results of Make Poverty History:

2005—which was the main year for the campaign—is over. Agencies and all those who participated are looking back… And they are saying, 'Did we get all that we asked for; did we get the aid; did we get the debt cancellation; did we get the trade for the communities that need it?

And when we are looking back, we sometimes look at the figures. We sometimes look at the decisions. But the most powerful thing about Make Poverty History is the numbers of people who got to know about how decisions made by so few affect so many.

✛

Chapter 7

Shaking the holy ground

Armenia is an ancient enclave of faith, but the people's historic beliefs have been tested in recent times by natural forces. Arshak Manukyan is among those restoring hope to his homeland.

People thought their homes would collapse any minute. Weakened walls and ceilings made most buildings dangerous to live in. For many near the Armenian-Azeri border, these houses were their only assets. Tragically, most residents did not have the means to carry out vital repairs. The earthquake of 2005 had shaken them to their core in this historic heartland of Christianity.

Arshak Manukyan was among those who came to their rescue. He was part of the Earthquake Response project initiated by World Vision Armenia in the north-eastern Gegharkunik region of the country. Arshak mobilized community members to renovate damaged homes around their small village of Tretuk.

This father of seven is tireless in his desire to help his people become prosperous. His own hands are cracked and scratched. The wounds are the result of long hours of hard work spent in the cold wind blowing from the snow-covered mountains that surround this impoverished and isolated community. Arshak wakes up before dawn every day and works through the night to provide for his children. His feet are barely covered with worn-out shoes that fail to protect him from the biting cold of the Armenian winter. Temperatures can be bitterly cold from December to late February.

Like many other Armenian families living in rural areas, Arshak is struggling to make ends meet. But despite countless difficulties and challenges, he is committed to seeing progress for his tiny community.

Growing up in a large household with eleven siblings, Arshak began working to support his parents' household when he was only seven. He was combining school studies with taking the neighbour's sheep to pastures, cutting grass and cultivating potato fields. In addition to his growing responsibilities, after graduating from high school, Arshak continued his education in Russia, learning to operate a tractor. Following his two years of army service, he returned to Armenia and married 23-year-old Geghetsik, his classmate and a childhood friend.

Their life ahead was promising, exciting and full of opportunities, but when the Soviet Union fell apart in 1991, so did the country's huge industrial enterprises. Arshak's family moved to Eraskhavan in southern Armenia, hoping to find a better living. He recalls:

At first when my family arrived at Eraskhavan, there were possibilities for making a living. I had a job in the collective farm. I was also employed by the railway station as a labour worker. Usually after completing my daily work at the collective farm, I was going to the railway station to load or unload the railway wagons.

The collective farms were privatized, however, and Arshak lost his job. In addition, the railway where Arshak was working stopped functioning. All railway lines to Armenia were blocked by Azerbaijan due to the conflict over the ancient enclave of Nagorno-Karabakh. Arshak describes the situation:

Losing both my jobs forced me to find different solutions to continue providing for my family. I started farming to be able just to provide enough food for my children.

I was hoping to bring my family out of poverty when we decided to move to the community at Tretuk. But I realized soon that I had to work very hard to make a living no matter where we were, because the situation was similar across the country.

He began working as a carpenter, electrician, tractor operator and a night guard at the local school—all at the same time. He was doing his best to feed the family and provide for his children's basic needs.

Arshak's family moved to Tretuk in 1994. They were among hundreds of other refugees who were displaced during the war with Azerbaijan over Nagorno-Karabakh—one of the former Soviet Union's most intractable and long-standing conflicts.

Legally speaking, the tiny republic of Nagorno-Karabakh lies within Azerbaijan's borders, but most of its inhabitants are ethnic Armenians. Like many others during this post-Soviet period, the Manukyans were not sure about the direction their life would take in the new era. They were isolated from the rest of the village because of their refugee status and poverty. But after more than a decade spent in Tretuk, Arshak is the one who people turn to whenever they need help. How times have changed!

Looking at Arshak's frail and skinny frame, it is hard to believe that he can endure life's countless difficulties and still keep a cheerful and loving outlook. His bright smile lights up his sky-blue eyes. 'I never wanted to leave my village,' he says, 'although many people went away searching for a better life.'

That determination to stay and help his community became stronger when World Vision Armenia started its development projects locally. 'When the World Vision team visited us for the first time,' says Arshak, 'people didn't believe that someone was going to help us because our village has always been forgotten.'

It did not take long for Arshak to understand that World Vision Armenia had come to stay—and to make a difference. He started talking with his fellow villagers, persuading them to co-operate with their new friends to improve the local situation. The World Vision team were amazed at how inspired Arshak was to help, while also taking care of his large household and holding down four jobs at the same time.

Because of his active involvement, Arshak was selected by his fellow villagers as a member of the Community Active Group (CAG). They were responsible for maintaining the link between the community and World Vision Armenia, identifying the needs and finding solutions.

Before the earthquake of 2005, the only essential belonging that Arshak's family had was their home, but as a result of the earthquake they lost even that. The quake lasted seconds, but it was enough to cause severe damage to the 1960s building. The stone and mud structure just wasn't strong enough:

When I saw the damage made to the house, I thought that my family would have to move to another place. But we had nowhere to go to. The whole community was shocked and hopeless.

No one in our community could even think that organizations from abroad would address our needs and respond to them. But when we heard that World Vision offered to help us rehabilitate our damaged houses, we were nicely surprised.

Many people, even then, did not believe that the initiative would actually happen and that the houses would be restored. But that changed when the first truckloads of construction materials arrived. Arshak says that it was the first sign of hope they had seen in ten years. 'It was unusual to see somebody share our misfortune with us,' he explains. 'Now we see that although we live far in the mountains, we are not alone in this world.'

However, the earthquake response was not easy at first. Arshak had volunteered to mobilize the community members to take the initiative for construction works. He was later appointed as warehouse keeper by the Gegharkunik ADP (area development programme) staff. Arshak formed a team of eight people from among his neighbours, which went around the village renovating the houses damaged as a result of the earthquake.

But when World Vision Armenia's truck with construction materials arrived, no one showed up to unload it. People were busy with harvesting and other chores. So it was left to Arshak and his wife Geghetsik to unload the truck. They allocated one room of their small house to store the construction materials for the whole village. Arshak explains his attitude: 'There are disabled people like Vanik in our village, who cannot do anything themselves to improve their situation. Those of us who are healthy and strong by God's grace should be responsible for the weak ones.'

Things have moved on, however, and as a result of Arshak's and his fellow villagers' efforts, Tretuk has changed beyond recognition. The old cracked walls have been rebuilt, providing people with strong houses that will last for generations to come. 'I thank God every day that now my children have a safe and warm place to live in,' says Arshak.

In addition to rebuilding houses, World Vision Armenia launched a pig-breeding project to help people increase their income-generating opportunities. Arshak was appointed by the community to be responsible for taking care of the mother sows and for the fair distribution of piglets to other villagers.

People trusted that Arshak would make the best decisions and choices not only for his family but also for the entire village. According to the villagers, there were many times when Arshak considered the community problems as top priority, often at the expense of his own needs.

As a result of World Vision Armenia's projects, Arshak's children, along with many others, benefited from quality medical care and received warm clothing, shoes and school supplies. This helped some of them to go back to school. Arshak's 14-year-old son Vardan was one of the children who returned to school after spending almost two years working in the fields and doing other odd jobs to support his family.

There are still many needs in the Manukyan family, but the love and respect the family members have for each other often compensates for their lack of material wealth. Geghetsik, Arshak's wife, works hard, despite the cost to her health of living and labouring in this troubled place. 'We've been through a lot of difficulties,' she says. 'There were days in the past when there was no soap in the house to wash the children's clothes.'

Looking around Arshak's house, where the walls are still waiting to be cemented and the cold wind blows through the cracks in the floor, it is sometimes difficult to understand the source of their strength and the reason behind the broad smiles.

For Arshak, though, the answer is simple. 'I thank God for my family every day,' he says. 'I am very proud of them. I live for my children and do everything I can to support them and teach them about the true values of life.' Arshak's hopes for his children's future are boundless but, amazingly enough, they are within the limits of the village of Tretuk:

This village is a lost corner and we virtually live on top of the mountain. But I know that in four to five years, our village will be doing much better because of World Vision and with our own participation as well. I love my village very much. I will do everything that I can to help it become prosperous, because I want my children and grandchildren to stay here.

Armenia has not always been a forgotten corner. It boasts one of the oldest civilizations in the world. Its borders used to include Mount Ararat, which biblical tradition identifies as the mountain on which Noah's ark rested after the flood. Now located in Turkey, its peaks still remain a national symbol of Armenia.

In AD301, this land of rich history and rugged terrain became the first nation to embrace Christianity as a state religion. According to tradition, the Armenian Apostolic Church was established by two of Jesus' apostles, Thaddaeus and Bartholomew.

Now the land's welfare is left to the new disciples like Arshak. They are the ones who will help Armenia regain its strength and retain the culture, traditions and values for future generations. People like Arshak serve in a humble way that may often go unnoticed, but their hidden deeds touch many lives, leaving meaningful and lasting footprints on this ancient landscape.

Chapter 8

Knocked off my feet

From serving packaged food to well-off Westerners to
designing aid programmes for poverty-stricken Africans,
Tristan Clements is on an amazing journey.

*If you're not living on the edge, you're taking up too much space. (Anon—
as seen on a ski poster)*

He was stacking milk at Sainsbury's. He was told that he was an
outstanding employee, and the temp agency in Cambridge, England,
was delighted with his work. But the beeps of the checkout, the
clatter of supermarket trolleys and the chimes of piped music
became a soundtrack of discontent. Tristan Clements could pass his
own sell-by date if he didn't chase his dream.

From childhood, Tristan had a destiny. He knew he was born to
travel and to help others. Finally, at 26, that wish has come true.
Today Tristan works for World Vision in Niger, the second poorest
country on earth. He helps co-ordinate the compassionate response
to a year-long drought and locust invasion that have wiped out the
nation's farming industry.

That mindset was in his DNA from the start:

*My parents were English-born, but my father became the first member
of his family to go to university. He studied medicine at the University of
London. He then went to Canada for a year before spending a year
working for a Catholic mission in the jungles of Peru, where in his mid-20s
he ran a hospital in a small isolated town.*

He then went to New Zealand for a time before returning to the UK, where he met and married my mother. Within a few months of their marriage, they travelled overseas with Save the Children, first to Bangladesh and then to Afghanistan. They left Afghanistan a few weeks before the coup in early 1978, after a tip-off.

Tristan was born in January 1979 in the ancient city of Lancaster. His father worked as a paediatrician at a local hospital. They had only just celebrated their son's first birthday when the family was on the move again. They went to New Zealand, where his father got a job with the Ministry of Health. 'I grew up in an "international humanitarian" home, if such a thing exists,' says Tristan.

Six years later, his father joined the World Health Organization (WHO) at its headquarters in Geneva. The family spent two years in Switzerland, then they moved over the border 20 miles away to a village in France, where they lived for a further 15 years. Crossing the border was a daily routine for work and school. Tristan became literally attached to his passport:

My father travelled a lot with his work for the Expanded Programme on Immunisation (EPI). That involved his travelling to developing countries around the world to monitor their immunization programmes. He worked on the programme to eradicate measles. He was away four or five times a year, though never more than two or three weeks at a time.

Although he worked a competitive, stressful and important job, he never felt like an absent father. He left for work early in the morning, but was invariably home on the dot of 5.30 each evening for family dinner. And he never worked evenings or weekends.

Every two years they were granted 'home leave' to visit New Zealand. The trips included staying at other destinations en route, which meant taking in places like Australia, Thailand, Canada, Hawaii, Tahiti and Fiji. Those journeys remain highlights of Tristan's colourful childhood. He lost track of how many plane flights he had taken, but he was particularly impacted by a 24-hour visit to

Bangkok. 'Thoroughly intoxicated' by that one glimpse of the city, its exotic sights and smells haunted him for some time.

The family influence was key for this budding young internationalist. Just listening to their personal accounts was a powerful experience:

Some of my earliest memories growing up are of my father's slide shows of Peru, Bangladesh and Afghanistan. They were places far removed from my own experience. My parents were always good at helping my brother and me to understand that we lived an incredibly privileged lifestyle, though we wouldn't fully come to terms with that until we were older.

I watched my father come and go, each time to another exotic location —Uganda, Zimbabwe, Guatemala or Nepal. During the '80s he visited the Soviet Union and Communist China. In 1991 he travelled through parts of war-ravaged Afghanistan, facing landmines and ragtag militias. Each time he came back, I saw his pictures and heard his stories, and learned a little bit more about the world beyond.

The transformation was complete. A bright young visionary was ready to emerge. 'By my early teens,' Tristan recalls, 'I already knew that I would be a traveller—and that I wanted to help people.'

Even school offered training for his future destiny. Tristan attended an English-speaking International school in Geneva, where he was 'surrounded by kids like me'. He rubbed shoulders with the children of ambassadors, international financiers, UN officials and wealthy businessmen. This campus of 800 students represented more than 90 nationalities.

At the start of every school year, each class went on a field trip to a different European destination. In his later teens, Tristan went to New York to attend a Students' United Nations conference on the rights of the child. He also accompanied his church youth group to an event called Mission 96, which drew 7000 young Christians to the Netherlands. They slept like refugees in a huge, freezing warehouse. But the real impact came from listening to speakers from far-flung places. He returned home with 'a powerful sense' of wanting to get involved.

Tristan decided to focus on geography. He worked towards a BA at Cambridge, and followed it up with a Master of Philosophy in Environment and Development:

I studied issues of the developing world—courses on the Third World, on Africa, on the politics of Latin America, anything I thought would help me get 'out there'. My general 'travel and help people' ideal gradually sharpened into wanting to work with poor people in the developing world —not a particularly focused goal, but it drove me.

To gain some field experience, he met an ex-colleague of his father from WHO in Geneva. Ambrose Wasunna had started a small development project in the remote north of Kenya, and Tristan spent most of his summer there. He was shocked by Nairobi— 'a filthy, violent, poverty-ridden hole'. But his first trip to Kapedo, where Ambrose was running a hospital single-handedly, changed the way he saw the world for ever:

The inhabitants of the village, the Turkana, were in a low-intensity tribal conflict with their hill-dwelling neighbours, the Pokot, with periodic cattle raids and villagers left dead in their wake. We visited one of the villages that had been attacked and razed to the ground. The only building left standing was the old schoolhouse, which had been ransacked. Layers of anti-Pokot or anti-Turkana graffiti were plastered on the blackboards, just underneath the date still chalked in the top corner, eerily marking the last day lessons had been held there.

Famine had already gripped the area. Tristan can still remember seeing sun-bleached bones of cattle at the roadside, and he learned the meaning of hunger when their own food stocks ran low. He came back from Kenya thin and shaken, but with 'an ever-strengthening vision' of what he wanted to do.

Later, he watched the events of 11 September 2001 unfold on his TV at home. This only reinforced his determination to make a difference. He wanted to work for NGOs in the Third World, but had never held down a 'normal' job. That is when he signed on with a temp agency and ended up stacking milk in Sainsbury's.

Tristan realized that this direction was not going to be sustainable, and, in frustration, he blew his savings on a trip to New Zealand. For any other young person, it would have been an act of defiance against the system, but Tristan had a greater goal in view—though he did upset his temp agency by quitting. His parents had already moved to Melbourne, Australia, so he followed them there. Not surprisingly, he spent three months being rejected by temp agencies.

Tristan took on some voluntary work for a small NGO in Melbourne. His work impressed the managing director, a former World Vision operative. She suggested that he meet Geoff Shepherd, who was running World Vision Australia's Emergency Relief Team. They had a little work that needed doing around the office; they would even pay him. 'I would've done it for free,' Tristan recalls.

He started as a Progamme Assistant on a one-month contract, which rolled over into two more months. The job involved supporting Programme Officers with their 'portfolios'—their list of country-specific projects around the world. Tristan found the atmosphere intoxicating:

A couple of weeks after I joined as a Programme Assistant, the siege of Monrovia took place in Liberia. World Vision staff, among others, were being airlifted out of the city by US military helicopters while shells dropped in the city… Every couple of weeks, another of the four Programme Officers would be getting on a plane to somewhere exciting.

Andrew Lanyon, a few years older than me, had just come back from Iraq. He'd been helping to airlift emergency supplies, ahead of the US invasion. There were pictures on the wall of him helping to unload a cargo plane, and glossy magazine interviews and photos—our team's very own minor celebrity! He would go back out there a couple of months later and end up staying until World Vision closed its Iraq office down. I was overwhelmed to be part of this.

When the team's Communications Officer left, Tristan took over that role for the next six months. 'I was knocked off my feet,' he recalls. 'I was suddenly opened into a world I'd been wanting to get into for years.' He had to get in early each morning and find out from news agencies, NGO bulletins and World Vision office updates what was happening in the world of disaster relief. Then he would compile a brief for key World Vision Australia staff.

The Bam earthquake in Iran struck on Boxing Day that year, 2003, while most of the key staff were on holiday, so Tristan got a first-hand look at everything that was going on, both in World Vision Australia and the wider International Partnership. A couple of months later, three of the four Programme Officers left within the space of four weeks, and Geoff Shepherd invited him to take on that role.

Two months later, the Darfur crisis erupted. Tristan travelled with Geoff to eastern Chad, where 200,000 refugees were spilling over the border to escape conflict in Sudan. 'I have never seen, before or since, such a hostile place,' says Tristan. He also travelled to Latin America, weathered the tsunami nightmare in south-east Asia and, finally, when the Niger food emergency deepened in mid-2005, he was sent there.

He has since been upgraded from Programme Officer to Relief Programme Manager, which means co-ordinating all the World Vision emergency activities in Niger. World Vision is also looking to expand its work to include activities that will help mitigate any future food crises. But Tristan has had to come to terms with the fact that, sometimes, he cannot save everybody:

We visited an intensive care centre run by another NGO. They had run out of food, and there were about 25 mothers with their children there. Some of these children were horrifically thin—skeletal arms and legs, skin stretched tight over their skulls—every bit as horrible as the worst news pictures you've seen. They barely looked human.

We immediately started making phone calls and did what we could to get more food there. Food arrived two days later. We brought more in after that as well, and the clinic was stocked. But when we came back the next week, we found that three children had died in the intervening time. That can be hard to deal with.

However, he has seen many other children get better. Tristan explains that youngsters enter the feeding centres as skinny, listless creatures. But within just a few weeks of attending the programme, they gain weight and look much healthier. 'That's really encouraging,' he says.

He finds that just being able to do something is rewarding in itself. Tristan believes that working in emergency relief is 'definitely intoxicating'—seeing new and unusual places, travelling to beautiful locations and living such a varied lifestyle. He loves to hear stories from his workmates, and is 'continually humbled' by both the givers and receivers of aid.

When in Chad, he drove north with colleagues for eight hours until they were on the edge of the Sahara. Surrounded by low, rolling sand dunes, with clumps of dry brush, they found themselves on the border with Darfur, where Janajawid militia had been going across in raids.

They found about 20,000 Darfur refugees camped over ten kilometres of dry riverbed. The refugees had fled their villages, in some cases leaving family dead behind them, with their homes burned. They were living out in the open and sleeping under thorn bushes. These people would walk several kilometres to the village of Bahai, where they would have to queue for twelve hours to get water. Then they would walk back to their thorn bushes and settle down again.

Tristan and team stopped to talk, then returned to their air-conditioned land-cruiser for their journey home. A woman stopped them and chatted to the driver in Arabic. Someone waved a water bottle, and Tristan assumed that the woman was asking for a drink. Nothing was exchanged, and they drove on.

'Did she want our water?' asked Tristan. Their driver, Blandin, shook his head. 'No. She was trying to offer us a drink,' he replied. Tristan was profoundly affected by the encounter:

This refugee woman, who had nothing, who had to walk five kilometres and queue for hours to get her water, had such a strong sense of hospitality. She was willing to share what little water she had for her family with four strange men—even though our own vehicle had all the supplies it needed. That woman inspires me.

✢

Chapter 9

Their eyes speak more than any words

One of Europe's most beautiful locations was the setting for
one of its ugliest wars, but Jasmina Vazrupa is among
those restoring the land.

Jasmina Vazrupa still reels from the rifle butts that struck her head a
decade ago. She feels the effects of the blows whenever the weather
changes: 'I have terrible headaches and dizziness. Sometimes I can't
open my eyes for hours.'

During the time of the Balkans conflict, she worked as a translator for a group of journalists. They were captured by soldiers in
Vitez, a district of Bosnia-Herzegovina (BiH), who accused Jasmina
and her colleagues of spying. They released three people, but kept
two journalists, along with Jasmina. They dragged her to a base-
ment. There, they kicked her and beat her with rifles: 'because I
didn't want to admit that I was a Serb or a Muslim spy'.

In the meantime, the released journalists called for help from
some United Nations troops who were stationed not far from Vitez.
'They came to rescue me,' Jasmina recalls. But they were almost too
late: 'When they arrived, they found me on the floor covered with
blood. The first thing I heard was one of the UN soldiers saying,
"She is dead." As they were putting me on the stretchers, they
realized I was still alive.'

Fortunately, Jasmina lived to share her story. Now she is Zenica
Zonal Manager for World Vision BiH. Her homeland has become

divided into a joint Bosnian/Croat Federation and the Bosnian Serb-led Republika Srpska.

World Vision has been working there since spring 1994. At first, the team offered such assistance as public kitchens. Numerous relief and rehabilitation projects followed. By 1996, World Vision BiH was assisting more than one million people, many through a reconstruction programme for war-damaged dwellings. Following an end to the war, the focus shifted to helping people recover and move on.

Jasmina can remember what things were like before the conflict. She was born and grew up in a small industrial town, Novi Travnik. It used to be called 'the town of youth' because allegedly it was the youngest city in Central Bosnia. The town revolved around the big munitions factory, where her father worked. She was raised in a 'very happy family', with three younger sisters. They were very close and enjoyed an easy life with an abundance of friends:

In 1980, after I married, my husband and I moved to his birth town, Vitez. We lived there until the outbreak of the war. The life before the war in both of these towns was wonderful.

There were many cultural events going on every weekend, such as folk dance in the town square, drama plays in the open, and winter games. Since both towns are fairly small, people knew each other—and if you were in need, you knew you could count on your neighbours.

Then, in the 1990s, everything changed. Preparations for a new census, elections, and the separation of the Republic of Slovenia from Yugoslavia left many people bewildered and asking why. Then the demonstrations started. Jasmina already had three children, two girls and a boy. There were whispers of war, and fear was rising in people's hearts. Jasmina could not imagine a conflict even starting, but she sensed 'a great difference' in her community: ·

Serb neighbours moved away. Croats and Muslims started avoiding each other in the streets. Many of my friends left. Then in Vitez there was a small conflict between Croats and Muslims. That day I understood that war was inevitable. Yet what could I do? Nothing but wait.

Before the war, Jasmina worked for a major wholesaler, as a financial controller and then a manager. Then she and her husband started their own import and export company: 'But the war came and they took everything,' she remembers.

In September 1993 she and her family were displaced from their home. It eventually became a burnt-out ruin. The only thing they were able to take with them was their lives. They fled a short distance to a safer village near the industrial town of Zenica:

A relative of ours left for France, and we took his apartment. We moved nine times in one and a half years, going from one apartment to another. Soldiers or police were coming and moving us on because homes were reserved for soldiers, and my husband wouldn't join the army.

We were constantly living out of bags because we didn't even have a suitcase. My husband was conscripted twice and imprisoned once because he refused to join the army. I had to go and talk with a lot of high-ranking officials and finally convinced them to release him.

In return for his release, Jasmina's husband had to work as a volunteer. Jasmina herself started working for humanitarian agencies as a translator. There was massive displacement. Houses were looted and set on fire. People were imprisoned or killed: 'They were afraid for their lives. It was better for them to leave their houses than be found and killed.'

In 1994, a 'chance encounter' was to change Jasmina's life. She met Angela Mason of World Vision USA, who was setting up a new office there. She remembers the day well—there was heavy shelling in the town at the time—but she was impressed with World Vision's work:

I started loving what World Vision does because it focuses on children. After that, I worked for other organizations for a while but stayed in contact with World Vision. Sometimes I used to do translation work for them.

Then a friend of mine told me World Vision was looking for a Repatriation Officer in August 1998. The pay was half what I had been getting (with another employer), but I knew this was what I wanted to do.

Jasmina's first job with World Vision involved helping displaced people to return home. At one village, she found an old lady called Ana, who was weeping as she sat on the doorstep of her ruined house. Ana had been excluded from the rehousing list, as priority was given to whole families for refugee return. 'My family have abandoned me, everyone has abandoned me. Even God has abandoned me,' she said. Jasmina sat down beside her and responded, 'God hasn't abandoned you. Let's pray to him'.

After praying with her, Jasmina went away and found the engineers who had been assessing the houses. They discovered that there were enough cost savings on their estimates to rebuild an extra couple of houses. Jasmina says, 'I persuaded them to add Ana to their list. That woman was able to return home. She died only two weeks later. But she died in her own home—knowing that there is a God who cared about her.'

Jasmina has since progressed to becoming Zonal Manager, in charge of all the World Vision projects in the Zenica area. She is also the Christian Commitment Co-ordinator for World Vision BiH. 'I really love that work,' she says.

Despite the horrors of the past, Jasmina is also living back in Vitez, near Zenica. The steelworks is the main industry in Zenica but only employs a fraction of the workforce it used to have before the war. World Vision rents an office from the steelworks, because they have so much spare space now.

Jasmina's team is making a difference. In 2000, she was working on World Vision's CATH (Creative Activities Trauma Healing) project—just one of the innovative ways in which the agency reaches out to this war-torn land. The scheme was running in no fewer than 16 schools. In one of the schools, she met Sanela, an 11-year-old paraplegic girl from a village near Zenica. The head-teacher asked her parents to stop sending her to school because it was 'a nuisance' having her wheelchair in the classroom. Jasmina remembers:

You should've seen the tears in the eyes of this child when she was told she couldn't finish school. She was very talented, especially at painting.

At that time, World Vision was supplying new furniture to the school. I met with the director and I told him, 'If you don't allow this child to come to school, you don't get our furniture!' World Vision arranged to build wheelchair access for the school, so the girl could finish her education.

Bosnia is a beautiful country, with fairytale landscapes, ancient meadows and warm, welcoming people. Traditionally, children were raised to love their neighbours and to respect people from all groups and backgrounds. It was considered a privilege to have come from a mixed marriage. But the war has left a bitter legacy. Bosnia remains the second poorest nation in south-eastern Europe. There is high unemployment, and problems continue between ethnic groups. Jasmina tells us:

In the canton where I live, there have actually been even more segregated schools created during recent months—even though the law says they are not allowed to have segregated schools anymore.

I know one of the officials in the education authority. When we met in a group of friends and were asking each other what we had been doing, he said, 'Oh, I've been busy dividing schools!' I was so angry. I told him he should be ashamed of what his government department is doing.

The three main ethnic groups are Bosniaks, Serbs and Croats, but there are also smaller ethnic minorities. Roma—the indigenous 'gypsy' community—is the most marginalized group. World Vision runs a project to help Roma children to integrate into primary school and older Roma to complete their secondary education.

Many Roma children never enrol in school, and a lot of those who do attend drop out eventually.

In 2003, a 12-year-old girl, Jagoda, came to the project to say that she would have to leave school to get married. Jasmina was stunned. She tried to tell Jagoda she was not ready for marriage, and she should first finish her education.

'What about your dream to become a teacher?' asked Jasmina. 'What happened to that wish to be respected by non-Roma people?' Jagoda didn't answer. She just wept. Jasmina and her colleagues spoke to her parents and persuaded her father that it would be better to let Jagoda carry on learning:

Her mother still isn't convinced. She didn't go to school herself, and she doesn't see the value of it for her daughter. Jagoda is still coming to the World Vision classes. She told her parents, 'You can stop me going to the ordinary school, but you can't stop me going to our own class.'

World Vision runs a Children Emergency Fund to provide treatment for sick or disabled children that is not covered by the state health insurance. Various support offices have contributed over the years. Over the last year, this has meant that the team could help more than 50 children get the care they need.

Jasmina and her colleagues in Zenica give to the fund. The money they collect may not be a huge amount, but, as Jasmina explains, 'it gives us a great feeling when a desperate parent comes to ask for help for their child, and we are able to assist'. Even a token donation of 20–50 euros is enough to cover some medicines, nappies, or the doctor's visit. According to Jasmina, people are very thankful for what World Vision has done for their children: 'Their eyes speak more than any words spoken in any of the world's languages.'

Five-year-old Harun suffered from a progressive, debilitating brain disorder called panencephalitis. His mother, Aida, told Jasmina that he was born as a normal child, but suddenly, as a young boy, he refused to eat and spent a whole day sitting on the floor. Doctors said he needed to be treated in Cyprus. Jasmina recalls:

We made a payment of KM1000 [about £330] from World Vision's emergency fund and KM1000 from the staff contribution. That finally completed the desperate search for money, and Harun was sent to Cyprus.

After two courses of treatment, he feels much better. He started to eat and to spell out the first letters of his name. Harun's health problems are not over, as he still suffers from epilepsy, but his parents are not giving up hope.

Just as World Vision opens doors for others, Jasmina believes that it has opened one for her, too. She is able to get on with what she always wanted to do—helping people, especially children, and openly practising her faith. 'World Vision gave me an opportunity to be what I am,' she says, 'and what I love to be.'

She still suffers from her own war wounds, and one of her deepest desires is simply to enjoy good health. She has had to learn to live with the painful headaches that make up her own personal legacy from the conflict:

The most frustrating thing in all of this is that the soldier who had beaten me was, and still is, my neighbour. He asked for my forgiveness, and explained that he didn't know what he was doing because they (all soldiers) were drugged. They had been taking LSD. My reply to him was that I will forgive—but never forget.

Chapter 10

The people who touch the sky

The dramatic results of development work outweigh the
pressures and demands of just getting the job done—
as Marcos Quino discovered.

Sleeping under the stars on a clay-brick bed with animal skins for
sheets, he wondered if he had made the right career move. 'What
am I doing here?' Marcos Quino thought to himself. 'Did I study
that much for this? If my family gets to know about this, they will
mock me. As soon as I get back, I'll quit.'

Marcos had only just started at World Vision's field office in
Bolivia. His first trip had been to Laja, a town in the middle of the
cold, high plains of the Altiplano. Parts of the region are rocky and
barren, almost like a Martian landscape. When he left this desolate
place three days later, he wrote his resignation letter:

*I talked to the National Director. He explained to me in more detail what
the job was all about, what World Vision was all about—and that moved
my heart. I never gave her my letter.*

*It was my duty as a professional to serve these people... we had
opportunities they never had, so it was only fair to help them get the
opportunities they needed. So I stayed.*

Marcos was born in Oruro, north-east Bolivia. Formerly a busy
centre in the 1940s and 1950s, thanks to silver extraction, now it
can look like a ghost town. Only the February carnival breaks up the
monotony. Normally it's a passing-through place where miners get
their supplies and then return home.

At the time, Marcos' father was in the final stages of ministry training at the Baptist Church Seminary. He was one of the first ordained pastors to emerge from the ancient Ayamaras, the largest indigenous group in Bolivia. When that time ended, the family moved to La Paz, the country's legislative capital. Nicknamed 'the city that touches the sky', La Paz is located at 3600 metres above sea level and is surrounded by two chains of mountains. It's a growing city, boasting plenty of businesses and some modern and impressive buildings. Yet it is also surrounded by a belt of poverty, with poor neighbourhoods set up by those who migrated from the rural areas.

The fourth of eight children, Marcos was educated at the American Institute, a pioneering Methodist school with 100 years of history behind it. One of the oldest schools in Bolivia, at the time it was highly respected. However, tragedy struck the young family. Marcos' mother died when he was six. 'I have few memories of her,' he says. The children were raised by the eldest sister and a maid who became known as 'Mama'. Marcos describes his life at the time:

Since my dad was a pastor, he had to spend much of his time in the church. And since the pay wasn't enough for all of us, he had three extra jobs. So he used to come back home at 11pm almost every night. I still don't know how he was able to cope with that for so many years.

He was a primary schoolteacher, teaching music and religion. He also worked as a messenger/legal paperwork deliverer and used to do merchandising clearance with Customs. We learned to do everything by ourselves—cook, clean, fix the house and so on. We even spent our vacations doing household chores and fixing roofs and stuff at home.

An entire family of young children had to assume grown-up responsibilities and duties. Marcos' father promised them that he would not marry again until the last of his sons and daughters had at least graduated from high school. Twenty-one years later, he got married and had three more sons.

He was the family's spiritual guide and today is an active pastor at the age of 80. His constant message was, 'The best reward you can give me is to serve the Lord somehow; that's even better than school grades or diplomas.' The result? Most of Marcos' brothers and sisters are involved in some form of church leadership or activity.

Before going to college, Marcos noticed that his friends were afraid of military service, which is mandatory in Bolivia. With a cocky attitude, he declared, 'That's not a big deal' and decided to do it. He was in for a few surprises. He was posted to Achacachi and Guaqui by Lake Titicaca—the highest navigable lake in the world and one of South America's most enchanting sites. Legend says that ancient heroes emerged from the depths of this vast blue lake. But there wasn't much time to take in the view, let alone the mystery of it all. Living conditions were terrible, and the trainee soldiers had to work hard on potato plantations. In Marcos' own words, he 'touched reality'. He realized that while he had benefited from a quality education in an important city, most of his comrades were from poor backgrounds. Only a few were able to read and write:

I decided to teach as many as I could and formed a small group. This group was the slowest ever to learn, and I got scolded many times because of that.

But it was worth it. I knew that was the right thing to do. I learned to value people. I felt I was in the world to do something for these people, instead of wasting my life away.

After Marcos had spent six months in the army, a new lieutenant arrived at their camp. One day, he called the battalion together and made a strange request. He demanded to know how many of them were evangelical Christians.

Marcos knew there were probably 100 believers among them, but he was one of only five who stepped forward to declare their personal beliefs. The lieutenant told them to wait for him at his office and sent the rest off to have lunch. Marcos tells what happened next:

When he came to his office, we expected to be punished and reprimanded—or treated as worthless. It was difficult to profess a different expression of faith to the established Catholic church in Bolivia at that time. But he said he wanted all his soldiers to be strong and courageous as we were, and told us not to say anything to the rest.

Later on, we found out he was in the process of becoming a Christian himself, and our example had helped him. I was able to identify myself as a Christian, regardless of the fear of the punishment or trouble that might have caused me.

Marcos wanted to work for the church but realized that he needed to have some academic achievements behind him. Not even his studies were carried out in the most comfortable of environments, however. Military coups had become common in Bolivia at the time. Marcos and his peers had to sit their exams in the shadow of military raids. Sometimes soldiers were actually posted in the classroom to watch over them.

Intrusions into their studies became even more bizarre. For instance, their calculus tests included completely irrelevant questions such as 'What is your opinion about the military government?' Marcos explains:

Students were considered as Communists who should be deported. We couldn't tell we were students, for that was enough to be jailed. We marched and protested against military regimes, and many of our classmates lost their lives.

There were times when we had to flee from the university, climbing up the walls and then jumping down to the other side—boys and girls. Some of the girls couldn't make it, and we couldn't help them, either. I lost many friends those days. We never saw some of them again.

Eventually, the chaos subsided and democracy was restored. Marcos was able to finish his studies. He then started giving private lessons to rich young students, but his heart wasn't in it. He really wanted to serve the needy, so he went on to start a social programme at church. His aim was to help schoolchildren who were experiencing problems with particular subjects—

especially mathematics. He even secured funding for it.

As a young teenager, Marcos had heard about World Vision. In 1984, he found out that there was a vacancy at their Bolivian field office. Almost at the same time, there was an opening at the Bolivian Central Bank that interested him, so he applied for that one, too. Both institutions offered him jobs.

It was a dilemma. Marcos liked both placements, but his father helped him to discern the right way forward: go with a stable Christian organization that was serving the poor, or with an unstable financial institution with better money. Convincing himself that 'money isn't everything', Marcos decided to work with World Vision. One of his first tasks was to serve with a project in Laja—an assignment that almost put him off relief and development for life.

His next position was as Projects Promoter in Oruro. His team thought it would be a treat for him to return to his home town, but Marcos had only been born there and had never actually lived as part of the community. It turned out to be an inhospitable place for him, and he pleaded to be moved somewhere else.

Three months later, he was given responsibility for projects in La Paz and Pando, on the borderlands with Brazil. He enjoyed increased freedom and worked in the area for two years. Eventually Marcos became National Manager:

That [job] was made for me. I could really do what I wanted to do now. I felt uplifted and useful again. I got to know all the projects in the country and that enhanced my point of view.

I always gave my 100 per cent in all the positions I was in. And that was acknowledged by the institution—which was great for me—because my dream was always to give the best I could in everything.

Marcos has benefited in more ways than one by working with World Vision. He met a nutritionist and dietician called Esther, who had visited one of the projects as part of a church group. She later became his wife, and supports him in his role.

Marcos has made some remarkable inroads. In Santa Cruz, a

community leader rose up in opposition against World Vision. In a bid to become involved—and potentially close down the work from the inside—he climbed to the dizzy heights of becoming president of the board of one of the projects. Ironically, he became one of World Vision's best spokesmen, and even made a personal commitment to the Christian faith. 'He could have easily destroyed us if he'd wanted,' says Marcos, 'but he changed to become our best ally.'

In 1998, Marcos' team arranged for twelve classrooms to be built for a community on the outskirts of Santa Cruz. The project made a great difference for children who used to attend schools located far away (which had put many at risk).

Marcos believes that, like any organization, World Vision has had its ups and downs. Yet it has always maintained its Christian identity:

It has brought a social consciousness to the church. It has helped, by its own experience, to guide the church to this change from the temple to the community.

It has a different speech and different focus. Many NGOs do similar things, but World Vision has a biblical perspective. It's all about empowering the communities, to give them an active role in their fight against poverty.

He feels that the organization's work has resulted in transformation. Indeed, he refers to World Vision as 'a school of change'. The Bolivian team may not have reached 'multitudes' but, in his humble words, they have reached 'a few children'—and, as Marcos puts it, 'that will make a difference'.

Being a leader in development work is not easy. 'When I stay home for more than two weeks in a row,' says Marcos, 'my son and daughter ask me, "Why aren't you travelling this week?" But so far I've been with World Vision for more than 20 years. And if God wants me to, I'll stay with them longer.'

Chapter 11

Fighting the new apartheid

A far greater menace than racial segregation is threatening the
lives of countless South Africans, but people like Ledile
Mphahlele are fighting back.

Like most pioneers, Ledile Mphahlele was born at a crossroads. Her
birthplace was Pietersburg, a name associated with some of the
worst extremes of South Africa's history. Founded by the Voor-
trekkers, who were white Afrikaner farmers, the town was at the
start of many trading routes. It also became the location for a
concentration camp. But this wasn't part of the Nazi ideal—it was
built by the British to house nearly 4000 Boer women and children.

That same spirit lingered on under another guise, for much
later—when racial discrimination was institutionalized under the
apartheid laws—Ledile's own parents were forcibly removed by the
government. They were part of the process of separation that saw
1.5 million Africans shifted from cities to rural reservations. The
grim removals took place between the passage of the Group Areas
Acts of 1950 and 1986.

Apartheid practices were abolished in the 1990s, and today
South Africa is considered a middle-income, developing country. Yet
its people still face some harsh realities. Unemployment is at 37 per
cent, and it is estimated that 50 per cent of the population live
below the poverty threshold. Although 86 per cent of people have
access to some source of safe water, it is estimated that only 21 per
cent of households have piped water.

Pietersburg has been renamed Polokwane in an attempt to

exorcise the ghosts of a painful past and affirm the self-worth of the majority black population. But the surrounding area has a history of being 'peri-urban', because it lies at the interface between urban and rural. It's a crossroads. It's a place in crisis. Ledile tells us:

I grew up in both rural and urban areas. My father was a teacher, and whenever he was transferred from one area to the other, the whole family moved with him. This helped me realize that in rural areas there are people who are very poor.

My mother, who was a housewife, used to cook extra food so that we could share with our neighbours. She taught us that if you have clothes you no longer use, take them to people who need them. This had an impact on my life, because to date my home is always full of people looking for assistance or advice.

There were often poor relatives staying at the family's home. Ledile found it painful to see how their own immediate families were unable to provide the food and clothes they needed.

Ledile's family was Christian and middle class. She had the opportunity of going to good schools in the area. Her parents could afford to put her through boarding school and send her to university. 'I grew up with my three siblings and we are all university graduates,' she says.

She never had a problem with school—except for the long distances she had to walk. Initially, school was five kilometres away from her village. That meant waking up at 5am to prepare for a day of learning and have breakfast before she left home:

At school we had a feeding scheme which provided soup and porridge daily. At primary level, our mother tongue was used as the medium of instruction, and English and Afrikaans were taught as subjects.

This created a lot of language challenges as I progressed with my education, because at higher grades we had to be taught through English and Afrikaans.

These difficulties didn't stop Ledile from dreaming her dreams, however. While at boarding school, she used to see a classmate being visited by her elder sister, who was a social worker. One day, Ledile asked the visitor about her job. 'What impressed me most,' she recalls, 'was that she was helping the poor.'

Ledile wanted to do the same, so she set out to become a social worker, but her family wanted her to be a teacher. Her parents believed in teaching, as it was a family profession. Her paternal grandparents, uncles and aunts were all teachers. In her parents' minds, there was no other profession. Ledile recalls, 'It was painful for me not to pursue the profession I liked. I think that is why I could not remain a teacher for the rest of my life. I always want to help or provide solutions where possible.'

She went on to teach at high school for a year, and then entered teacher training college. She still looks back on some important lessons learned in those years, for she interacted with teachers in realistic situations that needed immediate solutions—such as seeing children arrive at school without uniform or food.

Sadly, Ledile's mother died in 1987. Ledile then found herself fulfilling the role of a parent, as her siblings were still young and at school. But the church played an important part in supporting her through this challenging time. As a result, her faith was strengthened, not weakened.

After twelve years of working at college, she joined an NGO called Media in Education. Her main responsibility was to train teachers on how to use multimedia in the classroom. Media in Education trains teachers on behalf of the government. When Ledile joined in 1997, it had a contract with the National Department of Education to train teachers on the new curriculum. After that, she joined the department herself, establishing centres for adult education.

Eventually she was drawn to a different kind of job that was being advertised in a newspaper. It changed everything. The ad was from World Vision. Ledile remembers, 'I knew the good work of the organization and its Christian values—hence I was motivated to apply… When I joined World Vision, I was scared, not knowing if I would be able to tackle the challenges I'd be faced with.'

Ledile was attracted to the work because World Vision was tackling the poverty, unemployment and pain of her people. Many of them were now suffering from the effects of a far greater menace than apartheid had been: they were living in the shadow of HIV and AIDS.

Although the killer virus attacked South Africa later than other nations on this vast continent, it struck with a vengeance. HIV and AIDS have been having a massive impact. The country has the highest number of HIV-positive people in the world—five million. Over the past few years, life expectancy has declined by nearly 20 years, infant mortality has risen, and the number of men and women in their 30s and 40s has decreased, yielding a sharp increase in the number of children left without one or both parents. Secrecy, fear, denial and stigma make it difficult to counter the disease.

Now among those fighting back, Ledile is managing an Area Development Programme (ADP) in the Sekororo area. The overall goal is to alleviate poverty, create employment and improve health, education and living conditions of the people in the region. In effect, she is tackling the apartheid that AIDS itself brings, as affected people are pushed to the margins.

Sekororo is located 70km from the town of Tzaneen in Limpopo Province. It lies at the foothills of the northern Drakensberg mountains and is surrounded by game farms and nature reserves. It is a rural region with low levels of access to services, and a high unemployment rate. A significant number of local people depend on state pensions and grants for income. Some are subsistence farmers, but they often lack knowledge of scientific methods of farming. Ledile and her team are helping them to improve on that.

One household she has been able to help is the Mathaba family. This is no ordinary family, for it consists completely of children. The group comprises five children who are also taking care of their late sister's son. The two youngest, Sabina and Ezekiel, are sponsored by World Vision supporters.

The family has been struggling financially because the only

member who is working is the eldest brother. He is a casual labourer with construction companies in Phalaborwa and within the ADP area. The children could not afford to build a house, so they had been living in a shack. The ADP provided ten packets of cement to encourage them to start building their own house. Project staff had also been helping them to register for government grants to provide them with enough cash to buy more building materials.

Three of the children are now receiving monthly grants, and part of the money has been used to buy the materials to build a house. The eldest brother taught the rest of the family how to make bricks, and they managed to construct their own home.

Ledile proudly tells the story of five women who were interested in farming. Her team and the village committee of Sofaya organized them into a group. The ADP provided them with fencing, fertilizers, seedlings and training. An officer from the Department of Agriculture gave them training and support.

As a result, the women are now growing chillies and vegetables. They call themselves Ikarabeleng, which means 'being responsible', and they have been selected as the best female farmers in the district. These kinds of stories continue to inspire and motivate Ledile in her work—as she calls it, 'the success of helping people to change their lives'.

At present, she is busy setting up drop-in centres that will feed and care for orphans. The ADP has trained home-based caregivers who visit households to support the infected and affected. To date, Ledile and her team have established six of these centres. She says, 'The ideal situation would be to provide the children with three meals at the centres. But at the moment, two centres provide breakfast and lunch while the remaining four are providing lunch only. The Department of Welfare provide stipend for the caregivers who manage the centres.'

In autumn 2005, American civil rights leader Jesse Jackson told South African churches that the fight against HIV and AIDS needed the same strength as the fight against apartheid. 'We must assault AIDS and stop AIDS from assaulting us,' he said. More efforts were needed, particularly in education, preventing the further spread of the disease. Jackson continued, 'We can fight AIDS by changing our minds and by changing our behaviour.'

Ledile is among those on the frontline, leading that fight. Already she has seen World Vision change its response from giving away handouts to empowering communities. Through the ADP, six communal vegetable gardens have been established, five income-generating groups set up, a pastors' forum created to help churches work together, and 3000 children cared for through sponsorship.

Yet the greatest challenges remain—poverty, and HIV's bitter harvest of an ever-increasing number of orphans. Those challenges are so great that Ledile even tackles the problems in her own time. Ledile is a committee member of an HIV/AIDS project at her local church. They started a programme to support a young woman who had declared her HIV status to the congregation. Ledile's hope for the future is to access more funds and be able to help people to unlock their potential: 'I want to see people being able to feed their families, to create a caring society which will be able to manage the situations created by HIV and AIDS.'

It has been said that what happens in South Africa matters for the rest of the continent. So the work of Ledile and others like her is significant indeed. They are helping to save Africa.

✝

Chapter 12

Priest of the muddy paths

Mihai Pavel survived the nightmare of Ceausescu's Romania
to lift others out of the darkness of poverty in his
troubled homeland.

The dark knights of Communism tried to extinguish the fires of faith in Romania. They transformed monasteries into craft centres. They forced priests into secular jobs. They rounded up dissenters and threw them into prison. But even the ruthless methods of the *Securitate*—the secret police of Nicolae Ceausescu's regime—did not succeed in stamping out every spark of belief among the vast Christian population of that troubled nation.

Father Mihai Pavel spent his entire childhood and adolescence in the shadow of that tyranny, but he survived the nightmare years of Ceausescu's government, eventually to become a leading light in World Vision Romania.

It was a hard road to destiny. His family had religious books that had been branded by the secret service as 'dangerous materials'. During the Communist years, it was a huge risk to keep such innocent-looking material, and even day-to-day living was a big challenge. Mihai recalls when he had to stay in long queues to buy gas cylinders so that his parents could cook. 'People were making lists with names at 2–3 am,' he says. 'Then we waited for hours for the truck with gas cylinders to arrive.'

He also had to cope with his own identity crisis, for Mihai was adopted and went for years without knowing who his biological parents were. He believed that God revealed the identity of his parents to him when he was 15. But his adoptive parents were humble, modest people. His adoptive mother was in fact his aunt. 'We were raised in a family of believers,' he says. 'My dad had an obedient nature and my mum was a real Christian.'

Towards the end of his adolescence in 1984, he met another man—a dentist—who impacted him in a way no one could have imagined. 'He changed my life,' says Mihai. The man used to attract young people into his circle. They met very often for a football game and talked about all kind of things. Mihai always knew that this unusual dentist had something special about him. Later on, in 1988, the 'dentist' revealed his true identity. He was in fact an underground Greek-Catholic priest, pursuing his mission illegally. Mihai says, 'His presence in my life had a powerful influence. It was like a sort of an abrupt "road to Damascus" experience. I then felt an undefined burning wish—without any specific target in mind.'

The young, inspired and impressionable Mihai decided to study at the Theological Orthodox Seminary in Neamt. His parents, especially his mother, were horrified at the thought, for in those days, many clergy were being jailed for their beliefs.

To make matters worse, Mihai became part of a secretive group of his own. There, he had the opportunity to meet priests who bore the marks of suffering from long stays in Communist jails. The group met every evening in one of the rooms of the Seminary. They discussed and debated various issues they were facing—particularly the problems they had to deal with during the Communist years. But they could not escape the surveillance society that was so much a part of Ceausescu's Romania. A worker from the Secret Service department used to come along, asking for a written explanation on the purpose of their meetings. Mihai explains:

Those who spoke one or two foreign languages were particularly asked to do that. We were asked if we corresponded with somebody from abroad, and why we were doing it.

But it was a useless procedure, as they already knew the content of those letters. All the letters that had my name as an addressee had already been opened by the time they reached me.

The purpose of the interrogations was twofold. The Secret Service wanted to recruit new agents, and to see if people were trying to undermine the regime.

Despite the interruptions, Mihai used his time wisely. He spent time meditating and read many books. He learned English, so he could consume even more literature. He found the joy of reading 'overwhelming', and the truths he discovered 'priceless'.

The church had become the final stronghold in people's lives. It was the place where they could go to become spiritually recharged and refreshed. It was the place where they could pray for the downfall of Communism—and their prayers were heard.

The Communist era was approaching its end, but no one actually thought they would see the Iron Curtain collapse. 'We had all tailored our lives on a certain pattern,' says Father Mihai, 'and we were not prepared for what followed.' Ceausescu's regime finally gave way under a series of violent events at Timisoara and Bucharest in December 1989. People passed from a system with very few options into another system with far too many. Mihai comments, 'I think the key word to best describe the post-1989 period is "troubled"—spiritual life included. That and a high risk of losing our identity.'

But the dramatic downfall of the Communist government resulted in fresh opportunities for Father Mihai. From that point he found a new path in life, rediscovering himself and his world in the process. Aged just 20 at the time, he realized that there were so many other things that people could read, listen to and enjoy, if they had the freedom to do so. Up to that point, the choices in Romania had been limited, to say the least:

I used to read only two newspapers—Flacara (The Flame) *and* Scinteia (The Sparkle), *the last one especially being a fervent promoter of Ceausescu's regime and the Romanian Communist party.*

After the 1989 revolution, we were witnessing an explosion of magazines and newspapers dealing with various subjects from politics to fashion and cooking recipes. It was a new world starting to open up to all Romanians.

Mihai entered the Theological College in Iasi, a city in the northeast, and started to look for new, enriching experiences. The first was a pilgrimage to Greece, as part of a group of young people from the Balkans. Then, in 1994, a colleague took him to see a presentation about World Vision. He knew nothing about the organization. After the first few lines, he felt as if he was listening to a totally different language. Everything was so new to him. Under the theme 'The Mission of the Church in the Contemporary World', the presentation was given by former Indian pastor and Vice-President of World Vision, Samuel Kamaleson. Mihai was won over.

In his third year of studies, the fledgling priest had an interview for a part-time job in January 1995. As a result, he started to work on the 'Village to Village' project funded by World Vision Austria. The aim was to bring together rural communities from Romania and Austria. Representatives from villages in both countries met to share experiences across a range of issues, from agriculture to economic development and education.

As a major result of their talks, the seeds were planted of the 'Help Children to Hope' community development programme that is presently taking place in Iasi and is now in its phase-out stage. But progress was hindered by a tide of scepticism, as Mihai explains:

Community development was a totally new concept for us—and we were trying to do that with people who had been cheated and lied to for more than 50 years. I was one of them as I had been raised on the same model.

I said to myself, 'World Vision is a job like many others. I will finish what I have to do, and after I graduate from university, I will leave the organization.'

But it did not turn out that way. As the Iasi Area Development Programme and other projects emerged, Father Mihai was keen to graduate—so that he would have more time to work with World Vision Romania. The organization started with relief interventions and child protection projects. Then it focused on rural Romania, where there were communities with complex needs. Ceausescu's regime had pursued a relentless programme of urbanization, forcing villagers into the cities while bulldozing their traditional way of life:

I remember walking through a sea of clay in one of the villages well known for its pottery craftsmen. I was wearing a pair of boots that Romanian soldiers completing the military service used to wear.

But the boot sole detached at some point because of the clay, and I had to bind the sole back using a string. My priest frock was always full of mud and clay at the end of a working day.

Father Mihai always felt he was not well enough equipped to tackle all the human needs around him, but he learnt as he went through different experiences. He and his colleagues had to improvise to cover the various gaps they encountered along the way. He started from a simple question: 'What would I do if I were a priest and had my own parish?' He found the answers through working in World Vision.

Mihai began as an office administrator, then moved to the position of Sponsorship Project Co-ordinator. Now he serves as National Director for Transformational Development and Christian Commitments. He says of his work:

World Vision is an organization that offers you many opportunities to learn. There is something very special about it. I was transformed on those paths full of clay. I still miss those years.

Jesus Christ is a real presence in everything we do. World Vision's message is the gospel message put into practice. World Vision is consistent to the gospel message and its mission to serve the poorest of the poor and the ones who have been forgotten.

These days, Father Mihai provides community development expertise and is responsible for the spiritual formation of his colleagues. He is an important contributor to World Vision Romania's national strategy. He combines his packed programme with a commitment to his own 'community development'—that of his wife and two young children (married priests are part of the life of the Orthodox Church). Mihai describes his wife as 'the silent, restless servant… she has a patient and serving attitude'.

When he first encountered World Vision, Mihai never dreamed of making a career there. Now he has become known as 'the priest of the organization'. He believes in what World Vision can do all over the world. He has seen the signs of change:

I went out to take photos for our annual progress report. I took a photo of a little girl, no more than five, who was living in a sheepfold. She had big, blue, beautiful eyes.

Years later, I met her again, by accident. She was a beautiful adolescent. Her eyes spoke to me. I recognized her and she remembered me. This is something I am always grateful for. It is a real privilege to see children growing and smiling in an improved context.

Mihai feels that World Vision workers should never forget they are there to serve the poorest of the poor. They are there to help those who no longer believe they can be helped—those who have lost all hope: 'World Vision goes out with a different message—the message that they can be helped and that God never forgets his creation.'

Thanks to people like Father Mihai, a new day is dawning in Romania. 'We are like candles that burn,' he says, 'leaving behind the memory of light.'

Chapter 13

Child of the killing fields

One of Asia's most glorious civilizations became one of the most terrifying. Molly Yos' story is one of deliverance from the horrors of the Pol Pot regime.

He had the air of a king about him. He was elegant and impeccably dressed and had a pleasing smile. Yet here was the man who had committed some of the worst crimes in modern history. That is how *New York Times* reporter Elizabeth Becker described Cambodian dictator Pol Pot when she met him in 1978.

Elizabeth was one of the few Western journalists to interview this infamous despot, who had been responsible for the torture and execution of millions of his own people. Her story appeared most recently on the BBC News website (20 April 1998).

One of those who fled for their lives from this horrific regime was Molly Yos. Molly now works as a Senior Operations Manager for World Vision Cambodia, but she spent part of her adolescence escaping from the 'killing fields' of the Khmer Rouge.

Molly was born in Prey Veng province in 1960. She was the ninth child in a family of twelve children, born of two mothers. Molly's father had remarried after his first wife died in childbirth, leaving behind five children. He was an official in the Ministry of Agriculture and supervised three provinces. In 1967, he was promoted to Supervisor of Provincial Agriculture in Cambodia, and the family relocated to Phnom Penh. Molly remembers:

I enrolled in a school near my new home in Phnom Penh. I quickly made friends with a girl by the name of Young Setha, nicknamed 'Eang'. She was from the village directly across the river from the Royal Palace in Phnom Penh.

We heard about an English class that was free. We wanted to be modern Cambodian teenagers who would not be referred to as 'a frog in a well' or 'boon cheroong' (square), so in 1972 we enrolled at the English school.

The programme was run at a youth centre run by mission agency OMF. Eang and Molly studied English using Bible texts. Molly was interested in Genesis because it answered many questions of life that she had wondered about since childhood. She began to believe in a Creator God and his Son Jesus. She started to attend Bethany Church, led by Chhirc Taing, an officer in the army of Lon Nol's Republic (since believed to have been martyred for his faith by the Khmer Rouge).

Molly took her sisters Sokun and Sotheavy to church, but it wasn't so easy to persuade her parents to attend. Since Sokun and Sotheavy had become sponsored children through World Vision, however, that helped to ease the concerns of her Buddhist parents. They knew that World Vision was a Christian organization.

Older brother Antipo was the first in the family to become a Christian. Molly remembers him preaching to the whole family, and receiving a beating as a result. In late 1974, Antipo shared his faith with Molly's two older sisters. They made a decision to follow Christ, just as Khmer Rouge artillery began to pound the city. They began to attend a floating church held in a large two-storey boat called 'Noah's Ship', which had been started by the youth of Bethany Church. But the Khmer Rouge were getting close, and there was fighting on the outskirts of the city.

Before long, expatriate missionaries were packing their bags and getting ready to leave. It seemed inevitable: it would be only a matter of time before the Khmer Rouge would overrun Phnom Penh. Pol Pot's plan was to evacuate the cities, closing schools and factories, and herd the population into collective farms. Intellectuals and skilled workers were being assassinated. Molly's missionary friends told her to be extremely careful about the Khmer Rouge catching her with English books, or even a Khmer Bible.

On 17 April 1975, the Khmer Rouge entered Phnom Penh. They began to execute people who were a part of Lon Nol's government. Many soldiers buried their uniforms and joined the mass exodus as the Khmer Rouge began to empty the capital. Those who were being evacuated to different provinces around the country were to be known as the 'new people'. They were to be systematically starved or worked to death, or they were simply taken away and never seen again.

Molly and her family tried to make their way back to their home village in Prey Veng. In departing Phnom Penh, they were separated from Molly's older sister, who was a patient in a mental hospital outside the capital. It was a difficult journey, to say the least. They made it as far as Kompong Trabaek (about 35km from home), then went into the countryside, where they built a little house of bamboo and palm leaves. Most of the family came down with malaria.

During this time, however, Molly's parents made their own Christian commitment. There was no medicine to fight the malaria, but Molly and her mother were taken to a very basic Khmer Rouge clinic to recover. After a few days, Molly's mother worsened and slipped into a coma. The family prepared to send her back to the village to die, but she eventually recovered and returned home in good health.

Spurred on by this breakthrough, the family began to read the Bible in secret, but soon even that became difficult. They had to bury their Bible for fear of being discovered and put to death by the Khmer Rouge. Then, they were hit by even more health problems. Tragically, Molly's youngest sibling, Sotheavy, contracted dengue fever and died. Molly remembers the horrors of that time:

My family and I were forced to plant rice and build paddy dykes in exchange for one bowl of watery gruel with a few kernels of rice in it. When I saw a dog pass by, it made my mouth water as I thought about roast dog meat.

Intense labour, with little food to nourish the body, made me become ill. I had constant diarrhoea and quickly became dehydrated and malnourished. They sent me to rest at a so-called 'clinic'.

The Khmer Rouge was preparing mass marriages in Molly's village. Her mother insisted that she come back from the clinic and take part. If she married someone from the village, she could live close to her mother. Molly wasn't thrilled with the idea, but eventually she went along with her mother's wishes and joined the group marriage ceremony, along with her sister Yos Em Sithan, in 1978. More than 100 couples were married that day. Molly and her husband now have three children.

On 7 January 1979, Vietnamese forces entered Cambodia after relentless border attacks and massacres of Vietnamese civilians by the Khmer Rouge. In a matter of weeks, they pushed the Khmer Rouge into the north-west corner of the country. Vietnamese troops allowed Molly and her family to return to their home village in Prey Veng, but they had to beg for food from their neighbours. In exchange for some rice to eat, Molly and her family worked the fields.

A new government was formed, called the State of Cambodia, led by Heng Samrin, Chea Sim and Hun Sen. They summoned Molly's father back to office. The family returned to Phnom Penh, and Molly went to work for the Ministry of Agriculture. It was 1980. But Cambodia was just a smoking crater, a fragile shell of its former self as the hub of south-east Asia.

Molly's father began to suffer from high blood pressure. When he died in 1988, a large funeral was held in his honour. All his government friends attended, as did members of Cambodia's 'underground church', but it was a huge undertaking just to arrange a Christian burial.

Sithan started working in the Ministry of Education and became well respected by her colleagues. An old schoolfriend had become the wife of the Minister of Cults and Religion, and she was able to arrange an audience with him. After the challenges they had encountered while arranging their father's funeral, Sithan and Molly asked the minister to grant freedom of worship. 'Under this regime, we have no right to worship in the tradition of our faith, no place to bury our dead according to our tradition, no rights at all,' they told him. 'This is not right. What can you do for us?'

They met with him on a regular basis, and shared from the Bible. The government minister even borrowed tapes to listen in his car going back and forth from work. He asked many questions and they answered. Molly continues the story:

On the last day that we were to meet, he asked us if Christians get involved in politics. I explained from Romans 13 that God ordains leaders of a country, and that Christians are encouraged to submit to and pray for their leaders.

I reassured him that Christians only wanted freedom to worship—not to stir up unrest for an already unstable country.

Eventually the minister made the first public announcement that Christians were able to worship according to their tradition. It was 1989, and at that time there were no more than 100 Christians in Phnom Penh.

Molly worked at the Ministry of Agriculture from 1980 to 1991. Like all government employees, she was paid in rice and fabric and was given a place to live. Then she was reintroduced to World Vision Cambodia through a British worker, Sally Shaw. Molly had already done translation work for the organization, in 1989–90.

World Vision had first entered Cambodia in 1970 in response to the government's international appeals for assistance, and remained until the siege of Phnom Penh. When World Vision re-entered Cambodia with the overthrow of the Khmer Rouge in 1979, only three of the original 270 staff members had survived the genocidal regime.

Molly started full-time with World Vision in October 1991. She was hired as a receptionist and inventory clerk until she was promoted to assist in the Operations Support Unit and then Staff

Development and Spiritual Nurture. She still remembers, with laughter, her first day at the office:

I was so scared every time the phone rang. I had never worked in such a modern office before. There were strange machines and many foreigners working at World Vision Cambodia then.

I was so impressed with the office. I took off my shoes as I entered the building. It was not until the second day that I realized everyone kept their shoes on.

On the Spiritual Nurture team, she helped create the World Vision Cambodia Holistic Witness Policy Paper, organized Pastor Fellowships, translated World Vision's core values into Khmer, led staff Bible studies and arranged retreats. In February 1998, she was transferred to Kompong Thom Operations, a three-hour drive directly north of Phnom Penh. There she ran the Spiritual Nurture and Leadership Programme and Staff Development, which were really two full-time jobs.

My family all moved to Kompong Thom. We started to raise pigs, chickens and cows. I figured that if I was to understand the poor, I had to start living like they did.

I even learned to care for the pigs myself. After so much work, I sold a pig and barely broke even. I realized then how difficult it is for people to make a living like that.

A year later, Molly was promoted to Operations Manager. After a time in Kompong Thom, she decided to return to Phnom Penh. Now she works as a Senior Operations Manager for the South Zone. A typical day would see her serving on various committees, such as the Gender Task Force and Leadership Team, alongside managing a large team of development workers.

She has seen many changes at World Vision, as the team serves a country that is not only emerging from a recent traumatic history, but also trying to survive as one of the poorest countries in the world.

Most of the children, families and communities in Cambodia's 13-million population live in desperate poverty. They struggle to meet even the most basic needs of food and clean water. Yet they are forging ahead to build an improved future for their families, their community and their country—and Molly is committed to helping them:

I want to be a part of helping to develop Cambodia. The three years, six months, and 20 days of Pol Pot's regime have left us with so many horrific memories.

God helped me to live through the war and I will work to serve him in return. I hope that World Vision Cambodia is able to restore the values and self-esteem that were lost during that era.

Chapter 14

Make my life count

It was a warts-and-all story about a pioneer for the poor. Marilee
Pierce Dunker wrote of her own family's experience, and changed
countless lives in the process.

*Let my heart be broken by the things that break the heart of God. (Prayer
by Bob Pierce)*

Anchelee was lying on a mat in the middle of the floor. She drifted
in and out of consciousness as her immune system disintegrated.
She was too weak even to sit up and talk to the people from World
Vision. They had come to see her at her parents' shack next to one
of Bangkok's canals, for Anchelee was dying from AIDS.

Her nine-year-old son was sitting at her feet, tears streaming
silently down his face. Anchelee's visitors felt they should leave. It
was a moment for mother and child. But one of the workers pulled
the little boy on to his lap and began to rock him. As soon as he felt
the comforting arms around him, the boy let out the most heart-
rending wails they had ever heard. 'The rest of us were all just
weeping with this child,' said one of the visitors, Marilee Pierce
Dunker. She continues:

*I looked and saw that the mother—who I thought was so far out of it—
shaking with silent sobs for the child. So I went over and laid my hands on
her, and the team leader said, 'Pray.' We were in a Buddhist home and the
name of Jesus had never been spoken in that place. I didn't want to offend,
but when it's time to pray, it's time to pray.*

We started praying, asking Jesus to comfort this woman and fill that place, take away her fear and pain—and bring peace. When we were done, the leader came over and started talking to her, and as he spoke, my eyes were just locked on Anchelee's. I watched her eyes—which were so glazed over with pain, suffering and fear—and all of a sudden I saw a flicker of hope.

Marilee discovered that the woman had received a gentle message about a God who loved her. After returning home to the US, Marilee checked on Anchelee's condition. She was holding on, and had since made her own decision to follow Christ. Marilee says:

That to me is the epitome of what World Vision does. We don't preach from the pulpit very often. We don't hand out tracts. But at the moment when it counts, our staff are there. We have the word of life when the heart is willing to receive it—and lives are changed eternally.

That story is one of many that Marilee can relate from her work with World Vision, although she calls this particular incident 'one of the great treasures of my experience'. She has been a child sponsorship advocate for World Vision in the USA since 2002. She has a unique qualification for her role, for Marilee is the daughter of World Vision's founder, Bob Pierce. Even so, visiting programmes across the globe and seeing them first-hand has been quite a revelation for her:

I walked around for about a year and a half with my mouth open. People would say, 'Close your mouth, Marilee, you're catching flies.' But I was so astounded at how big World Vision was and all that we were doing. Once I got comfortable, they asked me to do very much what my father did, and I just love that. It's telling the stories, making these children real, giving them names and faces and helping people to relate to these children in the reality of what they experience.

Of course, Marilee could tell a story or two already. After all, her family had lived the story ever since the work emerged from Bob

Pierce's remarkable revival ministry. In her book *Man Of Vision* (Authentic, 2005), Marilee explains how people would crowd forward to respond to her father's evangelistic messages at churches across the United States in the 1930s and '40s. On pioneering preaching tours of China, he saw huge waves of people deciding to follow Christ. In South Korea it was the same: 'like a dam bursting' is how he described the response.

One of those visits indirectly led to the formation of World Vision. Bob had spoken at a girls' school on an island off Amoy, China. Many pupils became Christians. He encouraged them to go home and tell their families what had happened.

A little girl returned to school the next day with open wounds. Her father had beaten her for announcing her newfound faith. 'This little girl did what you told her to do and now she has lost everything,' said the school principal. 'So what are you going to do about it?' The question caused Bob to donate his last five dollars to the school, and spurred him on to even greater things.

Bob was first and foremost an evangelist, sharing preaching arenas with people like Billy Graham. The most important thing for him was to see people making a decision to follow Jesus, but there was more. One of his favourite sayings was, 'You cannot feed a starving man's spirit until you've filled his stomach.' He adopted a practical approach to the gospel, and urged others to do the same.

As someone rooted in the evangelical wing of the wider church, known more for a greater emphasis on personal piety than practical action, Bob was ahead of his time. He had developed his own twin-track theology, marrying conversion with compassion. Marilee explains her father's viewpoint:

Today we call it a 'social gospel' or 'humanitarian effort'—but it really isn't. Jesus role-modelled it. When the people were hungry, he fed them. When they were sick, he healed them. When there was need, he met the need. And by doing so he engaged them immediately in the power of the gospel. What my dad saw was that people were hungry for spiritual truth. But the reality is, until you feed their stomachs, until you meet their physical need, people are not in a position to grasp spiritual reality and move on. We earn the right—we don't assume we have the right—to share our faith.

Marilee and World Vision were born in the same year—1950. The aid organization started life from a tiny office in Portland, Oregon, and went on to become a leading world charity responding rapidly to major disasters—but it became the more demanding baby. Bob's devotion to this growing and successful ministry cost the family dearly. Marilee's mother Lorraine had to cope with 'marriage by correspondence'. From the jungles of Formosa to the streets of Belfast, his schedule never let up, and neither did he. He was travelling for most of the year. The family lost count of the times when they would stand at an airport gate, searching the crowd for a glimpse of this 'man in perpetual motion'.

Years of 18-hour days, sleep caught on planes, unsanitary food and everlasting jetlag began to take their toll on Bob. His temper worsened, and his marriage buckled under the strain. His older daughter Sharon took her own life at 27. His health as well as his home life gave way, and he was diagnosed with leukaemia. Bob died in 1978, but the family was reunited a few days before. Their 'night of miracles'—an emotional gathering in a hotel room—is retold in Marilee's book. It is a moving account of an epic moment in their lives.

Her 'warts-and-all' log of the family's journey leaves no stone unturned. The grit and the glory, the pleasures and the pains, are all described in detail. Marilee's open and honest account continues to encourage and enlighten Christian leaders and missionaries the world over:

I wrote it the year after my father passed away. I was 29. My husband and I were on the pastoral staff of the Church on the Way, which is a big church in the United States, with Jack Hayford. I'd never written anything significant before. I'd done some little stuff for the church, but didn't consider myself a writer by any means. We had always said that when God heals our family—after seven years of true heartbreak and feeling pretty hopeless about the interpersonal relationships we all had with my dad— we're going to stand on the rooftops and shout and let the world know that God is faithful.

So I really felt led, and I say very carefully that God called me to write the book. But I do believe that he did, because otherwise I don't think I'd have the abilities to write it—and I found it quite easy to write. It just flowed. So it's one of those things where you know God's just writing through you. I wanted my father's life to end on a note of praise, not defeat.

When Marilee started out on her writing project, her aim was to give credit to God for restoring her family before her father died. To research the story, she moved in with her mother for a whole year. Lorraine would talk, Marilee would write, and then they would discuss their findings. But she realized that she had had no idea of the 'rich and amazing story' behind her parents' journey of faith. Marilee describes the process as 'a work of translating memories'.

Fortunately, Lorraine had kept all the letters that Bob had written to her from his tours around the world, so Marilee did not have to guess or imagine what her father had been thinking. His correspondence said much of it, offering valuable insight into his perspectives, in his own words. 'It was almost like having Daddy there to answer my questions,' she says.

I was just enthralled by what I was hearing… My idea of who God is and how powerful God is, just grew as I heard this story—the importance of things like prayer, the impact and the power of prayer in my parents' lives; my mother's tenacity to believe God and not waver and not give up… This is how they lived their lives. And that spiritual heritage was a huge gift. I learned what the story truly was and began to understand all of the rich spiritual lessons and revelations. Somebody called it a cautionary tale. It's a vital story for anyone preparing for ministry.

To this day, Marilee still hears of people whose marriages and ministries have been radically changed after reading her book. The vulnerable mixture of miracles and mistakes seems to touch a nerve with many readers. She has even had phone calls in the middle of the night from people who have been affected by the text. After reading the book on a plane, one man sought out her number. He phoned from New York to say, 'I couldn't go home before I called to let you know how this book has blessed me and impacted me.'

Once, Marilee was invited to a small gathering at a friend's house to meet some missionaries from Siberia. They talked about the couple's work. As the conversation went on, someone let it slip that Marilee's father had founded World Vision. All eyes turned on her as one of the missionaries said that her book saved their marriage and restored their ministry—all because she told the truth. Marilee comments:

Nobody bothered to tell me you weren't supposed to tell the truth. I was my father's daughter. He told the truth. How can you give God glory if you don't understand the battle? How can you understand how impossible things are and what God did if you don't understand how broken things were?

I am totally for letting people see the brokenness and the needs so they can appreciate how incredible God is—to restore, then resurrect and use. When the book came out there were definitely two factions. There were the people who went, 'Oh my goodness, what has she done!' and there were the people who embraced it and said, 'Thank you.'

Meanwhile, Marilee gets on with her work for World Vision. She overflows with stories from her trips, and from her father's early pioneering days. Those who engage in conversation with her can see how some issues have changed while others haven't. For instance, the fight used to be against leprosy: now it's also against AIDS. Some of World Vision's earliest work was with prostitutes and street children, and that same work goes on. The ageless gospel still grips people and gets them involved.

That involvement includes a number of celebrities who have added their names to World Vision's list of activists. Marilee talks proudly of links with Bono, the crusading singer of Irish rock band U2, with actress Patricia Heaton from the hit comedy series *Everybody Loves Raymond*, and with well-known country artist Garth Brooks. But it doesn't matter who you are or what you have been through, as her own story shows. Everyone can play a part, as Marilee explains:

I've experienced enough of God's surprising grace in my own life to see what he can do in a very ordinary 50-something wife and mother. He has taken me out of my comfort zone and given me the opportunity to really see him work through me in a way that makes a difference.

I believe that's the yearning of every single heart: 'God, make my life count, help me to make a difference.' I think God's more than willing to do that, but it doesn't just happen. You really have to seek it and be willing to pay the price. To get out of the norm. Try something new. Do something uncomfortable. And if you're willing to do that, I think God will surprise you.

✛

Chapter 15

A table in the wilderness

When disaster strikes, Eric Kiruhura responds—by setting up
an office. He gets the information flowing when
everything else has stopped.

The destruction was unimaginable. Buildings had been flattened.
Cars and buses had been picked up and thrown to the ground.
Bodies in bags were piled up on the pavement. Some corpses lay out
in the open.

World Vision teams had arrived just after the tsunami at Banda
Aceh on the northern tip of Sumatra. They had never seen anything
like it. They certainly hoped they would never see such a sight again.
Those were some observations made by videographer Tom Costanza
when he visited the area at the end of 2004. With the stench of
death in the air, World Vision workers handed out rice, noodles and
high-protein biscuits. Counsellors offered emotional support to
traumatized children.

On the distribution team was a man named Khasmir. The tsunami killed seven of his family members, including his father,
mother, brother and sister. His was the most dramatic description of
the disaster. He said that the wave approached as a black wall of
water about 30 metres high: 'It looked like a big, black cobra.' He
went to work at World Vision because he wanted to help others,
hoping it would make him forget.

Eric Kiruhura was among those first World Vision workers to
operate in the region straight after the disaster, but his job was to
distribute information, rather than nutrition:

The Indonesia Tsunami Response grew fast. I arrived in Aceh in the very first days after the tsunami had hit. There was an influx of staff and with it came demand for ICT services—not only in Banda Aceh but also other zonal offices that were sprouting up in other affected areas.

I was there for three months plus. I literally felt like I'd been thrown in at the deep end… this was my first major humanitarian emergency. But I received tremendous support and guidance from my leaders.

Eric had to supply computing equipment, internet connectivity and knowledge management. The task was overwhelming. He had to move fast, make quick decisions and provide a rapid provision of services. He recalls:

We had to work long hours to meet the demands in all locations. I remember flying one afternoon by helicopter to Lamno. I literally did the IT set-up of the whole office during the night and had to catch another scheduled helicopter in the morning to Meulaboh.

I did the IT set-up during the day just in time to catch another scheduled helicopter in the evening back to Banda Aceh. But God granted all of us strength to serve in Aceh.

The whole experience turned out to be an important memory for Eric. His formal title is ICT Specialist for the Global Rapid Response Team of the Humanitarian & Emergency Affairs within World Vision International. His responsibility is to respond to emergencies by setting up ICT systems within 72 hours of a major humanitarian emergency taking place. That might be in the form of voice or data needs:

This would be provision of internet connectivity for communication with support offices (fundraising offices) and partnership office (global co-ordinating office).

I would also be expected to provide telephone services, mostly with the use of satellite phones, as most public phone systems are either non-existent or could have been destroyed by the disaster.

He is also responsible for creating a flow of relevant and timely information to decision makers. A typical scenario would find him quickly creating a temporary working office with printers, copiers, a local network, scanners, desktops, laptops, servers and other equipment and utilities.

In stark contrast to such a work environment, Eric enjoyed something of an idyllic childhood. He was born in Nakuru, Kenya. His mother worked in national parks for the Kenya Wildlife Service. He describes his early years:

I always looked forward to school holidays. My mum would pick us up and we would live with her in whichever National/Game Park she was assigned at that time.

We did stay quite often at Amboseli National Park. This is a lovely place to visit. I vividly remember the park teeming with thousands of wildlife as we would take a game drive with Mum on park patrol.

Eric was not able to live with his mother all the time, however. She was often assigned to areas that did not have easy access to schools, so he spent much of his early childhood living with his grand-mother. Grandma was a hard-working woman with an administrative role in her church, which meant an influx of church visitors to her home. She didn't have much, yet she always made sure there was tea for those who called:

She seemed to know everything. I had numerous questions to ask—and she had answers to most of them. But she was also a tough lady who would not tolerate nonsense from an energetic and mischievous boy.

She used the cane when necessary, and I am glad she did not spare the rod. She was loving and especially protective of me. Everyone knew I was Grandma's darling.

Eric recalls one particular incident. Ugali (maize/corn meal) had been served. All the older people dug into the mountain of steaming hot food. Before the young Eric could make a move, it was all gone.

It was like a little picture of the way the world often works. He noticed, however, that Grandma had kept quiet the whole time, silently observing the feast. She had kept some food aside, and handed it to him.

This wise old woman also introduced him to church life:

At that tender age, I played a small traditional drum in church. I also got baptized at the same local church. For [Grandma], being a follower of Jesus Christ was ultimate.

My personal spiritual journey can be traced back to early childhood days in the village with my grandma, and how I engaged in the local church… it was a good seed planted in me.

His fledgling faith grew at Christian Union and Scripture Union in the various schools he attended over the years. Eric made a conscious decision to be a follower of Jesus while at St Augustine's Preparatory School, Mombasa. School wasn't always easy, however. This was in the days when corporal punishment was commonplace. 'Making a simple mistake would see you being caned until your bottom was sore,' says Eric.

He wondered about the worth of a good education. Many older boys married before their 20s and started families, creating bigger households than their parents had. The cycle of poverty would roll on relentlessly:

It seemed that school was a boring and sometimes painful way to pass time. For me, it was more exciting herding animals, as I would get to play with other children. But I am glad for my mum's and grandma's visionary insistence on going to school. I have tremendous respect for these two women.

Another grown-up who had quite an influence on Eric was Mr Mlewa, his headmaster at St Augustine's. 'I was quite inspired,' says Eric. 'He made school a home and lovely place to be.' Mr Mlewa was interested not only in the children's education but also in their general well-being. He knew each pupil by name, visiting them in the dormitories or dining hall to see how they were getting on.

There was a matron to check health issues, a cook to make well-balanced meals, elderly women to check on cleanliness, and a boarding master to check on discipline and progress. School became a home from home:

While this might be common in boarding schools in mainly developed countries and private boarding schools in Kenya, it was revolutionary for a public boarding school in Kenya.

Educational results showed the success of this kind of system. St Augustine's did well in national examinations and continued to send a greater number of pupils to coveted secondary schools in Kenya.

Eric spent many school holidays with his mother, staying in Amboseli National Park, Samburu, Tsavo West National Park, Malindi Marine Park and Shimba Hills Game Reserve. He was influenced by his mother's passion for wildlife and conservation issues. Eric learned to respect indigenous communities and the environment and to invest in the well-being of future generations.

He completed his education at a leading high school in Nairobi. Starehe Boys Centre and School was unique, set up with the aim of providing free, high-quality education to disadvantaged street children in colonial Kenya. Eric remembers:

High school life was fun and yet challenging. There was lots of academic competition because the boys who made it to the school were all bright. We got to interact with students from all parts of the country and learnt to live with each other. Each boy was a brother and was treated as such. There was no tribalism whatsoever.

We were encouraged to be all-rounded people. Academic success would not be enough. Discipline, courtesy, responsibility, respect for authority, extra-curricular activities, spirituality and many more were needed to mould us into 'total men'.

Eric realizes now that such teaching is not common in many schools, either in Kenya or abroad. Many people have since been to Starehe to see how it works, including visitors from England's own royal family.

Starehe opened up a whole new world. Eric had dreamed of becoming a pilot, but when he took the high school's IT course, he instantly 'fell in love' with computers. Information technology offered new opportunities. 'I wanted to be part of them,' he says.

Taking part in a student exchange programme with a school in Canada was another eye-opener. Eric saw first-hand how Western education was lacking in areas of discipline and respect:

Very young pupils would tell off a teacher and manage to get away with it. Pupils would call teachers by their first names as though they were peers.

A student would question a punitive measure being meted out to them and would, at some points, have the audacity to refuse to do it. A student would storm out of class. The list is endless.

And this was a conservative school!

Though shocked at school life, he was impressed by general standards in Canada. 'In comparison to my own country, things worked,' says Eric. Roads did not have potholes. The streets were clean. People had access to medicine, hospitals and clean water in their homes.

Eric returned home believing that, with the right leadership in place, there could be positive change. Kenyan society could function like a well-oiled machine if it chose to. Canada had enabled him to catch that vision.

Eric went to university to study for a Diploma in Management Information Systems, but his family could not afford the course, so he had to find a job that would help pay his way. He applied to a number of NGOs. While following up on his contacts, he phoned World Vision's Sudan/Somalia Programme Office in Nairobi. They had a vacancy for an intern. Eric tells us:

I did a bit of research on World Vision and loved many aspects of its work—especially its Christian commitment and focus on children. When this temporary position came, I jumped on it, although I was told it might not translate into long-term employment. The rest is history...

World Vision was an answered prayer.

The organization paid for some of his studies, and some of its senior people agreed to serve as mentors. Eric lived and worked from Nairobi for a couple of years, and has since relocated to Dubai with his role on the Global Rapid Response Team. The work takes him across the globe:

I've felt welcomed into a community of Christians who not only have a passion for the things of God but also their work and ministry. For many World Vision employees, it is not just any other job, but a calling. This has rubbed off on me.

The Global Rapid Response Team is like a virtual family... the team is diverse in ethnic and social background—and even their brands of Christianity vary. But it all works.

✢

Chapter 16

Hope in the highlands

Mapuii cares for drug users and sex workers in the hilly
north-eastern corner of India. It's hard graft, but the results
can be life-changing.

She has had her bag stolen at least ten times, and she knows who
the thieves are. They are among the very people she has been
looking after at a day care centre in the north-eastern corner of
India, yet not once has she pressed charges.

Lallawmzuali is a nurse by profession. She is also a dedicated
World Vision worker who is always willing to walk the extra mile.
Mapuii, as her friends call her, goes above and beyond the call of
duty:

*In the day care centre different clients come and drop in… More then ten
times they have stolen my bags—sometimes including assets from our
project. I did not make any noise about it, because I feel pity on them as
they have become so desperate and uneducated.*

*I realized that I didn't really understand their situation. Instead of
taking any action, I prayed for them and talked with them. They confessed
to their deeds and they became closer to me, and they never repeat their
mistake. Whenever we show them love, they never misbehave—they
become good supporters.*

Mapuii serves the drug addicts and commercial sex workers of the
green and mountainous region of Mizoram. She has learned to laugh
and cry with them over the past six years of working with World
Vision. She looks after a group of women. The centre offers them

counselling, education on HIV, AIDS and sexually transmitted infections, safe sex practices and personal hygiene, through group work and one-to-one interaction. Daily devotions enable the team to share scripture and pray with the women.

Amid these complex life stories, often it is the simple things that mean the most to Mapuii, such as seeing a smile on face of the person she counsels:

Whenever I meet any clients, I see in them their emptiness, desperation and their need for love, care, support and guidance… I really feel happy to see my clients' lives being transformed from a drug addict or sex worker to becoming a normal person, attending church and seeing them accept Christ and become a useful member of the society. I feel happy that I am a part of God's plan in their life.

Mapuii lives in Aizawl—'the Land of the Highlander'—which is the capital of Mizoram. Standing on a high ridge bounded on the east by a deep green river valley, and protected on the north by craggy hills, it stands like a high citadel. The region's population is barely a million, and most of them are Christian. That is a result of British missionaries reaching out to the 'Mizos' in the 19th century. There are also stories of revival from early in the 20th century.

More recently, some of the Mizo population made the news because they were claiming to be part of a 'lost tribe' of Israel. Hundreds of them had emigrated to what they believed was their promised land in the Middle East.

If the tourism texts are to be believed, Mizoram itself offers a touch of paradise. It has a variety of landscapes—hilly terrains, meandering streams, deep gorges and bamboo groves. The people practise hospitality as part of their ancient culture. People's economic status is low compared to other parts of India, however. Mizos practise what is known as 'Jhum Cultivation'. They slash down jungle, burn trunks and leaves and cultivate the land. Many live below the poverty line.

Mizos enjoy close-knit communities, but the high unemployment rate drives frustrated youth to indulge in injecting and peddling drugs. Illicit substances find their way over the border, and young people are easy victims. Some of them become sex workers, which results in high percentages of HIV-positive among the youth. There are no opportunities for life skill education and proper vocational training to engage their interest.

Into this exotic, challenging mix came Mapuii. She was born on Christmas Eve 1979 at Kawnpui, Churachanpur, in the state of Manipur. She was the second youngest child of a Christian family, with one brother and two sisters. Her father was a hard-working farmer. Her mother wove local clothing to support him. Mapuii recalls:

With my mother's encouragement I attended Sunday school. On many occasions I was awarded with prizes for regular attendance and for doing well in my exams. Church was not a priority at all for my father, but my mother is a true Christian and would tell us stories from the Bible.

I attended a Catholic primary school and shifted to a less expensive school because my parents could not afford it. I remember there were games, a lot of singing, and teachers taught us how to pray. Apart from this, I used to help my mother at home with the housing chores and also helped her to weave.

During her school days she was an active member of her church choir. Mapuii got through high school and later joined an auxiliary nursing and midwifery course at the Regional Institute of Paramedical and Nursing, Aizawl. She successfully completed the training in October 1998.

She was good at athletics, such as long jump and volleyball. 'So my ambition was torn between becoming a sports personality and a missionary doctor to help people in need,' she says. But due to poverty, and the lack of infrastructure or initiatives taken by the government, she could not pursue her favourite pastime, so she ended up as a nurse—'to serve people in need':

After completing my nursing course, one of my tutors told me that World Vision was in search of volunteer nurses. I didn't know much about World Vision those days, yet put forward my application anyway. Later I was asked to join the organization. I think God answered my prayers.

Mapuii became part of her local World Vision team in 1999. Initially she worked as a part-time nurse, looking after 20 injecting drug users at a given time—caring for them, dressing their wounds, giving motivational counselling and home visits.

Previously, Mapuii had been indecisive about her career, and job offers from the government were tempting. 'But,' she says, 'when I saw my fellow youth who are drug addicts suffering from their wounds, helpless, outcast and discriminated by the community, I thought, "This is the place where God wants me to be."' The health centre offers abscess management to reduce pain from needle wounds. It provides counselling and awareness programmes among addicts, schools, churches and community leaders.

However, it has not been a smooth path for Mapuii:

At the beginning of my work among the injecting drug users, my family and friends used to tease me. But now they give full support and pray for me.

Being a young woman myself, people would stare at me while conducting street-based and outreach programmes. I used to feel shy, thinking that people will look down at me—but God gave me the strength.

The team also run an 'aftercare' programme. They enrol their re-habilitated clients for job skill development training in a new trade. Day care is offered for drug users and sex workers, which also acts as a referral unit to hospitals. Free medical care and treatment of basic ailments and infections are given to people living with HIV and AIDS and other sexually transmitted diseases. Mapuii explains:

When young people cannot afford quality intoxicating drugs, they opt for proxy drugs sold at slashed prices. Later, these drugs cause abscesses and all kinds of diseases. Young addicts come here in need of help and rehabilitation. If left untreated or uncared for, they will develop serious complications and ultimately die without knowing the truth about life.

The clients I work for need care, love and support in their life, as they are also created by God in his own image. It is my duty to show God's love by working among them. Many of them are homeless, and their families have given up on them because of their practices and behaviour.

Mapuii has experienced many challenges since working at the centre. She and the rest of the team have had to deal with families who refused to care for their drug-addicted children. They have also cared for children whose parents have then blamed the centre for the child's drug addiction problem.

She feels particularly discouraged when clients return to old habits. 'Whenever I am faced with such problems,' she says, 'I share it with my colleagues and pray to God, and I find my strength and carry on with my work.' A profound kind of job satisfaction keeps people like Mapuii committed to their work:

When I see the suffering who do not have the care of their family or community, I empathize with them. When they share their stories, my heart breaks. I want to help them as much as I can.

When they first come to the clinic for abscess treatment, it is shattering to see the suffering they have to bear as a result of their injections. The wounds cause unbearable pain. But after receiving regular treatment at the clinic, their wounds show improvement, and they begin to have hope.

Watching those kinds of changes taking place in her clients encourages Mapuii to keep going. 'When family relationships are restored, jobs are secured and they start attending church and leading a normal life, I am happy,' she says.

It is clear that Mapuii becomes emotionally involved with those in her care. 'I cry with them; I can't help it,' she explains. 'I think they do what they do because they do not know the truth. Most of the girls have the same fear—they fear they might have contracted HIV from their partners or husbands.'

Another source of inspiration that keeps her going is the stories of Bible heroes—in particular, the life of Nehemiah. That account inspires her the most because he was concerned for Jerusalem, took the initiative and rebuilt the city walls. So, she say, 'I continue with my work because I believe that God has placed me in this position to work with them, and to share with them his love and greatness so that they will one day be transformed.'

Amazingly, Mapuii also finds time to get involved in a local Presbyterian church. She serves as a Sunday school teacher, an executive committee member of the youth fellowship, a member of the evangelism committee, and in the choir.

Mapuii has seen World Vision's ministry grow in that region. When she first joined, it had few resources to carry out its work. She would have to use dressing materials from other centres and government hospitals. But now it runs two separate centres—one for drug users and another for sex workers. 'World Vision's ministry here has grown in commitment, work extension, staff capacity, building, information and technology,' she says. 'I hope World Vision will continue to be a channel of blessing and a peace builder, meeting the needs of the poor and oppressed, building community, working like a true Samaritan, glorifying God and working for the extension of God's kingdom.'

One final story sums up Mapuii's commitment to care, and how that impacts others. She was busy at work when a young man came in, looking for her. He was clearly in shock, not knowing what to say, looking frustrated and helpless. Mapuii asked if she could help him. He said 'No', but went on to tell her that he was plagued by doubts, so she decided to listen to his story. The encounter lasted for more than two hours. Mapuii says, 'He was blaming his Creator, parents, family—as well as himself—because he thought that no one loved him in this world and he had no hope in life… I told him that Jesus loved him as he is, but he never agreed.'

Before he went home, Mapuii asked the young man whether he

would come back or not. He said that a return visit would not be necessary. Even so, she said that she would pray for him.

Two days later, her visitor came back. This time he had a smile on his face. He said that before he arrived at the centre, he had had a blood test for HIV. The result was positive. Shaken by the news, he had decided to commit suicide. 'But he refused to carry it through because of the care we gave,' says Mapuii. 'After that, he came to day care and wanted to volunteer on our programme, live a normal life and educate his peers.'

Chapter 17

The chocolate man

Mark Grantham is not content with transforming communities from his wheelchair. He defies rough terrain and airline officials to visit them, too.

The guys that get their buzz from God will pick up a worthwhile spot of rejuvenation. They'll be, like, on a pig's back, busting with energy, loads to spare. Choice! (Isaiah 40:31, unauthorized Kiwi version)

He does the sweetest things. New Zealander Mark Grantham sells chocolates to raise funds for World Vision, and he conducts this unique enterprise from his motorized wheelchair, which he operates with a chin control. So far, his sales skills have scooped more than 20,000 NZ dollars.

Mark first started supporting relief and development work in this way when he was just twelve. Along the way, he discovered that he was actually good at the art of selling. The result? He turned out to be the best fundraiser in his school: 'I got into this because most people my age were doing a paper run to earn some pocket money, but I couldn't do that. Selling from my wheelchair was something I could do—and I wanted to be able to do something for someone else.'

Mark has many memories. He recalls a busker dressed as a clown, performing on the same patch. He was just a few metres away on one of Mark's early selling days in Newmarket, a busy upmarket shopping centre in Auckland City: 'He was rather annoyed with me because he reckoned I didn't have a permit.'

So how did Mark feel about that? 'Pretty downright disgusted,' he admits. 'I felt I could sell chocolate any way I liked!' Looking at the bigger picture, Mark was proud to be the school's top seller at the time: 'I felt good because I was helping my school—which was something I'd wanted to do for a long time.'

Later, he starting sponsoring a child through World Vision, and decided to carry on the chocolate selling. Mark's involvement accelerated even further. He now sponsors four children, three of them in India and the fourth in Tanzania. He has been impressed with World Vision from the start. 'World Vision helps many people,' he says. 'I want to contribute time and effort to supporting my sponsored children.'

Mark was born with cerebral palsy on 25 August 1976. He attended Kimi Ora, a special needs school in Wellington, Karori Primary School and Wellington College, a prestigious boys' secondary school. He recalls how his mother and father had to fight for his access to a so-called 'normal' education. It is a bold thing that some parents feel they have to do, if they take on their local authorities in that way. 'There was some kerfuffle getting into Wellington College,' Mark remembers with amusement.

Despite that, Wellington College was a highlight of his 'mainstream' schooling. One of the senior students who befriended Mark was prefect Perry Freshwater, a 'cool guy' in the First XV rugby team. With his attractive girlfriend on his arm, Perry took Mark out for dinner and a movie. 'It was great!' Mark recalls. Perry has continued playing rugby, making his debut for England in late 2005.

After the family moved to Auckland, Mark attended Mount Roskill Grammar for his remaining school years. But he didn't give up the chocolate selling:

Every year, the school had a work day when every student had to go out and get work, handing over their day's pay to help school funds. Every work day while I was there, I earned the largest amount, because I was good at doing it.

When I left school, at the final prize-giving ceremony I was presented with the Principal's Special Award for my fundraising efforts. It was given to me by local MP Helen Clark, later to become New Zealand's Prime Minister.

Mark's family have always supported his sales schemes. His father, Chris, who has a background in accounting, education and Christian service, recently took up a position as Church Liaison Manager for World Vision New Zealand. His relationship with World Vision began very much through Mark's involvement. He also saw how World Vision staff at all levels treated his son with appreciation and dignity.

Mark's mother, Jocelyn, was born in Tanzania, where her parents served as missionaries with Church Missionary Society (CMS). She teaches at an Auckland school for boys from difficult circumstances. His sister Rachel trained as a civil engineer but is currently working as a freelance photographer and gym instructor. She is married to Nathan King, former lead singer of popular Kiwi band Zed. Nathan is a World Vision Artist Associate, and has recorded his debut solo album.

Rachel remembers observing the prolific chocolate selling. As any younger sister would, she decided to try her own hand at her older brother's trade. So she started selling chocolates at school as a fundraiser. 'But I didn't quite have the knack,' she says, 'and I think I ate most of the profits! I only did it for a few months, but Mark has faithfully sold chocolate for the last 17 years. He has real "stickability" and determination—a lot more than most of us, who like life to be comfortable and straightforward.'

She credits her brother with having a generous heart: 'He's always been the more generous of the two of us—the one to share, to let me have the last biscuit, or to buy me the special Christmas present... Mark's selfless generosity, his patience and perseverance are inspiring and a constant challenge to me.'

According to his father Chris, Mark has always been persistent, too, and that has kept his parents on their toes. Chris says:

The nature of his disability meant caring for his daily needs as a child always took plenty of our time, plenty of energy.

If Mark had been content merely to sit quietly and watch TV, it might have been an easy option for us to leave him doing just that. But rarely did he let us have that option—his enquiring mind demanded to know what was going on in every sphere. He engaged in anything and everything he could.

Mark's strength of character has always propelled him into the 'mainstream'. Chris explains:

While Mark has always had many disabled friends and peers, he doesn't go for the isolation and segregation that society and bureaucracy un-wittingly (and wittingly) choose for 'the disabled'. And so some of his high schooling was fully in the mainstream, as are his recreational pursuits whenever he can.

Mark doesn't seem to relax from any of his responsibilities, particularly spiritual ones. When he was just 13, he was determined to show that he was serious about his Christian faith. He decided to be baptized. 'I wanted to get "dunked" to show my friends I was going on for God,' he says.

He knows how to answer those difficult questions, too—such as, 'Why does God leave you in a wheelchair?' Mark is sure of his answer: 'I'll be healed in heaven. I'll be able to run!' Recently he started attending Christian Life Centre in Auckland: 'It's a good church—I've made a number of friends there.'

Home is now a sunny, self-contained unit in Onehunga, a central Auckland suburb. The place is fully equipped for his needs, including wheelchair ramp, wide doorways and an electric hoist from bedroom to bathroom. Mark can live this way thanks to government funding, along with financial backing from his parents.

He has a support worker living with him, and his week is very full. The schedule includes Maori language class, Christian Fellow-ship for Disabled, wheelchair dance class, massage and music therapy. 'In the evenings, I like my own space,' he says.

One could never describe Mark as housebound. He proved that when he decided to make personal visits to his three sponsored children in Mumbai, India. Accompanying him was Matt Farrant, a long-time friend and a child sponsor who has worked in India. Hailey Amohanga, Mark's main support worker, completed the travelling trio for this epic journey. For most other people, this would be a major undertaking. For Mark, it was virtually 'mission impossible', yet he attempted it all the same:

For years I was planning this trip with my dad, who was going to take me. Six months before I went, Dad was in India on business and he sussed out wheelchair-accessible accommodation. He also checked out whether we would be able to get my wheelchair to the slums where my kids live.

Dad came back and said it would work. Then a month later his back got stuffed up and he had urgent surgery. I was worried that I might miss out on going to India, but my parents asked Hailey if she would go. She took it up, which was a great relief for me!

Mark had to take his manual wheelchair to India, as his motorized chair wouldn't have been up to the challenges of travelling, or negotiating small spaces or rugged terrain. People in India were very concerned about Mark's condition. 'Lots of people were always staring at me,' he recalls. 'I'm used to that in New Zealand, but in India it was more obvious, and adults stared just as much. But it didn't bother me.'

On check-in at Mumbai airport for the return home, he discovered that the airline was also anxious, wondering if they should be transporting him. Mark did not share their concern, however. He was doing what he had always wanted to, and, in the unlikely event of any medical problems, he could be helped by his friend Matt, who is a doctor. Everyone learns sooner or later that Mark is a very determined young man:

Hailey and Matt had to lift me every time we got in and out of the cars or vans. Getting the wheelchair down bumpy and narrow lanes wasn't very easy, or very comfortable! And when we got to the homes of my sponsored kids, the doorways were too narrow for my wheelchair, so I had to be carried in.

Such practical challenges appear to be secondary issues for Mark. His key concern is to appreciate the challenges faced by his sponsored children: 'If you haven't seen poverty, you don't know what it's like,' he says. 'I was very emotional and felt overwhelmed. They could see my struggle, and I could see their struggle.'

Mark continues to value his involvement with World Vision New Zealand and his relationship with the staff: 'I like to get really involved with World Vision. I recently spoke at staff devotions, and I've also visited the Australian and UK offices, as well as going to India.'

He also works as a World Vision volunteer at Parachute, a large, well-known Christian music festival. He showed there that he was as good at recruiting new child sponsors as he was at selling chocolate. For two years in a row, Mark got the first sign-up of the weekend: 'I talk to people and tell them they should sponsor a child. With 24,000 people at the festival it is a bit crowded, so I need help in getting around. And I have to stay offsite overnight because there is no wheelchair accommodation. Everyone is in tents!'

His activism takes many forms. He and World Vision International President Dean Hirsch together opened the new office in Auckland a year ago: 'I was very pleased to open the building,' says Mark. 'I helped Dean cut the ribbon.'

Mark inspires others, too. Moved by his story, international singer-songwriter David Lyle Morris composed 'Love Is Stronger Than Life'. David, who has worked with world-famous worship leaders Graham Kendrick and Darlene Zschech, is also a friend of the Grantham family: 'He likes what I am doing,' says Mark.

Onlookers must often ask the question, 'What keeps Mark going?' Certainly his Christian faith is a driving force for him, and he gets inspiration and encouragement from all sorts of people—from all walks of life. They include All Blacks legend Michael Jones, who is regarded as one of New Zealand's greatest rugby players. He has bought chocolate from Mark on a number of occasions. 'He encouraged me to pray that I would be able to sell more chocolates,' Mark explains. 'Then I can get more money and sponsor more kids!'

But what happens when the crowds have drifted away and the celebrity friends have gone to their next appointment? What motivates him then? 'The input I have into the lives of the poor,' says Mark. 'Knowing I'm making a difference. I know they're really poor. I wish I could do more.'

+

Questions for discussion and reflection

Our common humanity

Our common humanity: you and me; you, me and… them? We all have people we associate with and those we don't. We all have some inbuilt 'difference detector' that stops us from truly loving everyone. Through reading some of the chapters in this book, you will have encountered terrifying stories of violence and rejection that have stemmed from a misunderstanding of humanity. You'll also have found incredible stories of hope—stories like Sheila's and Jasmina's. You may wish to use some of the material below to discuss or reflect on what it means to be part of God's creation, God's humanity.

Colossians 3:12–14

Therefore, as God's chosen people, holy and dearly loved, clothe yourselves with compassion, kindness, humility, gentleness and patience. Bear with each other and forgive whatever grievances you may have against one another. Forgive as the Lord forgave you. And over all these virtues put on love, which binds them all together in perfect unity. (NIV)

+ What does the phrase 'common humanity' mean to you? What feelings does it conjure up within you?
+ After reading both chapters, what are your immediate impressions of Sheila (chapter 1) and Jasmina (chapter 9)?
+ How did Sheila and Jasmina differ from those around them? How were they similar?

+ Put yourself in Jasmina's place. Spend a minute thinking about what her life was like before the conflict and what it is like now. How does this make you feel?
+ Does Sheila's attitude surprise or challenge you? How does it challenge you?

Getting involved

Whether you look at the book of Proverbs or follow Jesus' practical teaching in Matthew 5, you can't help but hear the undertones of a drumbeat that Jesus calls us to follow, one that is invariably different from the drumbeat of the world around us. The following questions are posed to help you, or a group, consider the radical call of Jesus. Chapters 6, 8 and 17 each have stories of how very different people have responded to this call and the world around them.

John 15:11–15

'I've told you these things for a purpose: that my joy might be your joy, and your joy wholly mature. This is my command: Love one another the way I loved you. This is the very best way to love. Put your life on the line for your friends. You are my friends when you do the things I command you. I'm no longer calling you servants because servants don't understand what their master is thinking and planning. No, I've named you friends because I've let you in on everything I've heard from the Father. (THE MESSAGE)

✛ Spend a minute or two thinking about what sort of attitudes or obstacles stop people from helping others.
✛ After reading the stories of Mark, Rudo and Tristan, do you feel inspired to help others or trapped, unable to do anything for people in need? Why?
✛ In Mark's story, he says that while other boys were raising pocket money from paper rounds, he wanted to raise money for other people. How could you imagine raising money for others—and would you want to? What might stop you?
✛ Brainstorm ways that you could help people who live nearby, those who are considered poor in your town or city, as well as those who are statistically the poorest of the poor in places throughout the developing world.

Exclusion and persecution

Love may have been cheapened through decades of pop music and media but our need for love is central to life. Throughout Jesus' ministry 'love' is paramount, and yet, when we look around us, we see so much that is not 'loving'. From the struggles of a young disabled boy in Albania to the killing fields in Cambodia, the stories in chapters 2 and 13 speak of the world's need for love. Flying in the face of persecution and exclusion from society, these are stories of people whose love has changed the world around them.

Mark 12:28–31

One of the teachers of the law came and heard them debating. Noticing that Jesus had given them a good answer, he asked him, 'Of all the commandments, which is the most important?'

'The most important one,' answered Jesus, 'is this: "Hear, O Israel, the Lord our God, the Lord is one. Love the Lord your God with all your heart and with all your soul and with all your mind and with all your strength." The second is this: "Love your neighbour as yourself." There is no commandment greater than these.' (NIV)

✢ Which people are excluded in your workplace, school or where you live? Think carefully: what about disabled people, those who are culturally different or elderly, or who have less money?

✢ Do you see, or have you ever seen, any persecution? What was it? Why did it happen?

✢ Read Molly's story. How does it make you feel? Do you think that being a Christian makes you feel and think differently?

✢ What sort of difficulties would Kujtim have encountered in his life? Have you, or anyone you know, experienced anything similar?

✢ What can you do to help those who are excluded or even persecuted in your society? Find out what other people or organizations are doing in your area.

Prayer

We sometimes wonder at the words of Jesus in Mark 11. We can close our ears as he tells us that we can move mountains with a muttered prayer. And yet we hear almost unbelievable stories of answered prayer in other people's lives, in other cultures, somewhere else in the world. The reality of answered prayer can seem distant, or at least a little far off, for those very big requests, but Jesus' words still ring in our ears. Can they be true? Can they be true for us? Mihai's story in chapter 12 shows that the faith of the saints had a true bearing on a very big mountain.

Mark 11:22–25

Jesus was matter-of-fact: 'Embrace this God-life. Really embrace it, and nothing will be too much for you. This mountain, for instance: Just say, "Go jump in the lake"—no shuffling or shilly-shallying—and it's as good as done. That's why I urge you to pray for absolutely everything, ranging from small to large. Include everything as you embrace this God-life, and you'll get God's everything. And when you assume the posture of prayer, remember that it's not all asking. If you have anything against someone, forgive—only then will your heavenly Father be inclined to also wipe your slate clean of sins.' (THE MESSAGE)

✠ How does prayer make a difference in your life?
✠ Do you have an answered prayer that stands out in your memory?
✠ Can you imagine ever being part of an underground church movement, hiding from oppression? What would characterize your prayers? What would you pray about?
✠ Is there anything in Mihai's words on page 91 that stands out?
✠ What challenge is there to your faith? Are there small or even large things that you could or should pray about, which, if they were answered, would make a big difference?

What can one person do?

Do you ever feel as if there's something missing? You can work hard, try to please everybody and live life to the full—but there's still something that isn't quite hitting the spot. Jesus has a lot to say about this. He says that he came to bring life—life in all its fullness. It's not just a 'life to live until you die' or even just eternal life, but the fullness of life here and now. Both Ledile and Eric found fullness of life in the work Jesus led them to undertake as they served others around them (see chapters 11 and 15).

John 10:10

I came so they can have real and eternal life, more and better life than they ever dreamed of. (THE MESSAGE)

✛ What's the focus of your life at the moment? How does this affect what you do?

✛ Eric does a job that most of us can recongize, yet the environment in which he works is often very different. Is Eric 'living life to the full' or just living a full life? How would you answer the same question for yourself?

✛ Ledile's passion was to help her own people What sort of satisfaction does she receive from her work?

✛ Have you ever prayed that God would lead you to live life to the full? Spend some time quietly bringing your situation and life before God and asking him to show you how to live to the full.

✛ What changes could you make in your life that would allow you to live life to the full? Challenge yourself to do one thing—even one small thing—that you have been thinking about.

Calling

Lots of people talk about 'calling'; we may wonder if we will like ours! We can get confused when we try to discover what our calling is—attending this or that course, testing out different ministries to see if our passion really is juggling for the kingdom! We'll try anything once—often without any success in finding that one calling. But maybe it's as simple as following what's written in God's word or simply responding to the world around us. You can see how Marcos (chapter 10) and Mapuii (chapter 16) were both led to their calling by looking at the world through the eyes of scripture and responding to its needs. Use their stories to help you think through this sometimes difficult subject.

Ephesians 2:8–10

God saved you by his grace when you believed. And you can't take credit for this; it is a gift from God. Salvation is not a reward for the good things we have done, so none of us can boast about it. For we are God's masterpiece. He has created us anew in Christ Jesus, so we can do the good things he planned for us long ago. (New Living Translation)

✛ Have you, or someone you know, felt a strong calling to do something? What helped you/them to discover that calling?
✛ How does it affect your/their life day to day?
✛ What influencing factors helped Marcos and Mapuii decide to do what they do?
✛ How are their daily activities a response to the word of God and the people around them?
✛ How is your daily life building the kingdom of God? Write down your thoughts and book time out, one month ahead, to think them through and decide if you need to take further action.

Hope for a better future

What does hope mean? Is it different from faith? Hope is something that can shape our lives, yet it can be hard to explain. Throughout this book, stories of transformation show hope and faith in the face of difficulty or adversity. Rudo Kwaramba (chapter 6) has led a life pursuing her ideals of equality and justice across the globe while Marilee Pierce Dunker (chapter 14) has followed in her father's footsteps by telling the stories of the poor and marginalized. They are united in their faith that, one day, all injustice will end. Use their stories or that of campaigner Mayerly Sanchez from Colombia (chapter 5) to consider how hope has shaped their lives.

Hebrews 11:1–2

The fundamental fact of existence is that this trust in God, this faith, is the firm foundation under everything that makes life worth living. It's our handle on what we can't see. The act of faith is what distinguished our ancestors, set them above the crowd. (THE MESSAGE)

+ Through the years of frustrated relationships and disappointments, what do you think were Marilee's hopes for her family? How do you think she felt when circumstances changed for the positive? (See pages 106 and 107.)
+ In what ways are hope and faith different?
+ Do you hope for anything? Is it a hope for something this side of eternity, or the next?
+ Does your hope make you think differently about life? Would you live differently if you didn't have this hope?
+ Do you pray regularly for the fulfilment of what you hope for? Spend time now thinking and praying through your hopes and fears, bringing them before God.

Working towards a better future

Changing the world can sometimes feel daunting—an impossible dream. But it can happen. When we talk about making a difference, creating an impact in the communities we live in or even changing one person's life, we can feel a strange mixture of uplifting inspiration and guilt-ridden fear. The stories of Zoubeida and Ayalew in chapters 3 and 4 show that a little goes a long way, restoring and rebuilding something of God's kingdom on earth. Use the reflections below to think through how you can usher in the kingdom through your life.

Matthew 5:13–16

'Let me tell you why you are here. You're here to be salt-seasoning that brings out the God-flavours of this earth. If you lose your saltiness, how will people taste godliness? You've lost your usefulness and will end up in the garbage.

'Here's another way to put it: You're here to be light, bringing out the God-colours in the world. God is not a secret to be kept. We're going public with this, as public as a city on a hill. If I make you light-bearers, you don't think I'm going to hide you under a bucket, do you? I'm putting you on a light stand. Now that I've put you there on a hilltop, on a light stand—shine! Keep open house; be generous with your lives. By opening up to others, you'll prompt people to open up with God, this generous Father in heaven. (THE MESSAGE)

✢ Do you 'go public' with God? In what practical ways do you think you can do this?
✢ What does the passage mean when it talks about 'keeping an open house'? How are you being generous with your life?
✢ What inspires you about Zoubeida's story?
✢ All the way through the book, and in Ayalew's story in particular, there is an undercurrent of sacrifice. How much are you prepared to sacrifice to be salt and light to those around you?

✦ Share your thoughts with a local Christian leader and ask how their church community can be salt and light to the world around them.

Making a difference

Reading a book like this provokes the question, 'What can I do to help?' The answer is that for a small amount of time and money, you can achieve a great deal.

✢ Find out more: By visiting www.worldvision.org.uk you can learn more about how poverty affects the lives of people around the world and how you can help them fight it. Go to the *learn* section or click on *what you can do* to find out how you and your church can get involved.

✢ Make a donation: By making a gift you can help World Vision to bring support to communities and projects like those featured in this book. Visit www.worldvision.org.uk to make a donation or call the Supporter Helpline on 01908 84 10 10.

✢ Child sponsorship: For the price of not much more than a daily cup of coffee you could sponsor a child in a long-term World Vision programme in a country of your choice. Your financial help will take the community forward and your link with a child will enrich their life and yours too.

✢ Alternative Gift Catalogue: For an inspiring alternative to pre-dictable presents, World Vision's *Alternative Gift Catalogue* lets you 'give' friends and relatives things like chickens and pigs that actually go to some of the world's poorest people. Visit www.greatgifts.org or call 0845 600 6445 for your free catalogue.

✢ Use your will: Including a designated gift in your will is a way to bring hope and help to a future generation.

There are lots more ways you can get involved: just visit www.worldvision.org.uk to find out how you can help fight poverty, or write to World Vision UK, World Vision House, Opal Drive, Fox Milne, Milton Keynes MK15 0ZR.

A World of Prayer

Praying with Women's World Day of Prayer

Ed. Naomi Starkey

A World of Prayer is a globe-spanning collection of original and imaginative resources for prayer and praise, compiled from the annual services of Women's World Day of Prayer but suitable for use at any time of year. Representing ten countries from Guatemala to Indonesia, the book presents worship material on a range of different themes, such as caring for our world, healing and wholeness, and our response to God's calling.

Join in a retelling of the story of the prodigal son from Ghana; celebrate with the welcoming 'kava ceremony' of Samoa; share in dramatized prayers of intercession from Venezuela and the passionate call to worship written by the women of Lebanon. A short introduction to each country provides useful background information, while the book also has suggestions for use in both small group and wider church settings.

ISBN 978 1 84101 369 5   £6.99
Available from your local Christian bookshop or, in case of difficulty, direct from BRF using the order form on page 143.

ORDER FORM

REF	TITLE	PRICE	QTY	TOTAL
3695	A World of Prayer	£6.99		

POSTAGE AND PACKING CHARGES						
Order value	UK	Europe	Surface	Air Mail	Postage and packing:	
£7.00 & under	£1.25	£3.00	£3.50	£5.50	Donation:	
£7.01–£30.00	£2.25	£5.50	£6.50	£10.00	**Total enclosed:**	
Over £30.00	free	prices on request				

Name _____ Account Number _____

Address_____

_____ Postcode _____

Telephone Number _____ Email _____

Payment by: ☐ Cheque ☐ Mastercard ☐ Visa ☐ Postal Order ☐ Maestro

Card no. ☐☐☐☐ ☐☐☐☐ ☐☐☐☐ ☐☐☐☐

Expires ☐☐ ☐☐ Security code ☐☐☐ Issue no. ☐☐☐

Signature _____ Date _____

All orders must be accompanied by the appropriate payment.

Please send your completed order form to:
BRF, First Floor, Elsfield Hall, 15–17 Elsfield Way, Oxford OX2 8FG
Tel. 01865 319700 / Fax. 01865 319701 Email: enquiries@brf.org.uk

☐ Please send me further information about BRF publications.

Available from your local Christian bookshop. BRF is a Registered Charity

brf

Resourcing your spiritual journey

through...

- Bible reading notes
- Books for Advent & Lent
- Books for Bible study and prayer
- Books to resource those working with under 11s in school, church and at home

- Quiet days and retreats
- Training for primary teachers and children's leaders
- Godly Play
- Barnabas RE Days

For more information, visit the **brf** website at **www.brf.org.uk**